BEST DAMN HIP HOP WRITING

THE BOOK OF DART

DART ADAMS

Edited by
Amir Ali Said

Series Editor
Amir Said

Superchamp
Books SB

New York

Published by Superchamp Books

Copyright © 2019 Superchamp Books, Inc.

A Superchamp Books First Paperback Edition

Edited by Amir Ali Said
Arranged and Edited by Amir Said

DESIGNED BY AMIR SAID

Cover, Design, and Layout by Amir Said

Print History:
October 2019: First printing.

Best Damn Hip Hop Writing: The Book of Dart
/ by Dart Adams
Edited by Amir Ali Said
Series Editor Amir Said
1. Adams, Dart 2. Said, Amir Ali 3. Said, Amir 4. Hip Hop Music Criticism 5. Rap
Music Criticism 7. Music Criticism
I. Adams, Dart; Said, Amir Ali; Said, Amir II. Title

Library of Congress Control Number: pending
ISBN 978-0-9997306-6-9 (Paperback)

CONTENTS

FOREWORD   ix

INTRODUCTION   1

PART 1: CRITICAL OBSERVATIONS   5

Hip Hop Has Always Been an Inclusive Art Form and an
Exclusive Culture; Mainstream Rap Music Isn't   6

Hip Hop's Ever Growing Generation Chasm   12

1981: The Year Hip Hop Broke   21

1990: Rap's Forgotten Transition Year   28

1991: Rap's Other Forgotten Transition Year   39

How The Buzz Around Niki Minaj's Debut Demonstrates the
Rap Game Is On Steroids   49

The Quintessential Definition
of A Backpacker   54

PART 2: RETROSPECTIVES/PROFILES/REVIEWS   62

My J Dilla Journey: A Tale Of Two Jay Dee's;
10 Years Of Fandom vs. 10 Years Of Being A Dilla Scholar
(1996–2016)   63

From Unsigned Hype To King Of New York: The Improbable
Rise of The Notorious B.I.G.   71

GZA's Liquid Swords:
A 20th Anniversary Retrospective   77

"Fight The Power": The Full Story Behind
One of Rap's Most Important Songs   82

How Rawkus' Soundbombing II Launched a New Era of
Independent Rap   88

PART 3: PERSONAL ESSAYS   93

Glorified Bum   94
Dear Mama   96
I Can't Turn My Mind Off   102
Choices and Legacy: A Writer's Reflection
On His Station In Life   106

PART 4: FRESH PERSPECTIVES   110

Fans of the Internet Age: From Bravado to Emotion
and The Evolution of Rap Content from Mystique and
Mystery to Everything Laid Bare   111
Where's Hip Hop's *High Fidelity* and *Almost Famous*?
(And Why Brown Sugar Ain't It)   120
An Alternate Take on the Perception of Nas' *Illmatic*, 20
Years Later   127
Jay-Z Is A Business, Man: The New Rules for the Few In The
New Age of Rap Marketing   131
Tags, Throw Ups and Pieces: The Analogy Between Graffiti
Writing and Blogging   138
Odd Echoes of Bygone Eras: Why The Buzz of Odd Future
Was Real   140
17 Days In 1995: From the Drop of *Only Built 4 Cuban Linx…*
to the End of "Yo! MTV Raps"   145

CREDITS   151
ACKNOWLEDGMENTS   155

FOREWORD

The Importance of Music Education

Music is deeply embedded into our personal and collective existence. Music adds depth and dimension to our environment, it elevates the human spirit, and it contributes in many important ways to our quality of life. Moreover, music is one of the primary ways that we learn about ourselves and others. Music is crucial to our understanding of the different traditions and beliefs that exist in the world. And, of course, music is also one of the fundamental ways that we create and communicate in and draw meaning from the world around us. This is why everyone — regardless of age, cultural heritage, or socio-economic background — benefits from a diverse music education. Thus, the purpose of music education, and by proxy music education books like the *Best Damn Hip Hop Writing* series, is not only to inform but to enrich and enlighten us all. With music education books, people increase their awareness of rich and diverse cultures, beliefs, and societies; and they learn how and why almost nothing in contemporary society is created or communicated without the influence of music.

About the *Best Damn Writing* Series

There is a lot of good writing happening today. From the explosion of talented essayists to freelance writers to independent authors to DIY poets and more, this era is rapidly producing some of the most engaging and culturally influential writing ever published. At the same time, however, much of this writing is being missed by the very readers who would likely appreciate and gain from it the most. This is not to say that a lot of the great writing of today is being overlooked, but rather that the number of literary channels — and their outdated publishing methods and often non-inclusive traditions — is insufficient to the growing body of interesting writing that's taking place right now. And this is especially the case when it comes to contemporary anthologies.

Anthologies are a great way to discover new writers and a means for further understanding the art and craft of writing. For classic Western literature, the task of assembling an anthology tends to be a foregone conclusion, at least in terms of the writers (nearly all old white men) that readers supposedly should know. But I don't believe that contemporary anthologies need to suffer from a similar ideological, non-inclusive fate.

More specifically, the inclusive kind of anthologies — that I believe better serve new voices in writing — do not exist in tall order. Anthologies, which have typically been fashioned by a narrow group of people whose tastes are tuned to an even more narrow corner of writing, are often positioned well outside of the mainstream. Because of this, I think the potential of the anthology, as a pop culture item, is largely unrecognized. That's why I've created the *Best Damn Writing* series. I want to help anthologies become a more recognizable part of pop culture, not something merely for so-called literary types. Moreover, I want to reimagine what the anthology is; how it's shaped, who it's for, and how it works.

I think book anthologies are like music playlists for readers. And just like music playlists, literary playlists benefit from the specific tastes and backgrounds of its curators. Within this context I believe that there is a premium for curated literature that stands beyond bloated listicles or selection archetypes commonly found among literary elitists. I've cultivated my taste from a broad consumption of literature, music, film, art, and pop culture. Certainly, this is not to say that my taste is superior to anyone else's, but rather it's fine tuned to the areas of culture that I've long had deep interest in and, in many cases, that I have written extensively about. Thus, I want the *Best Damn Writing* series to be an anthology series that promotes some of the finest writing in popular culture, specifically in the areas of hip hop, poetry, film, memoir, art, and technology — all of the corners of culture that occupy my deepest interest and exploration.

As to what I believe constitutes the "finest" or "best damn" writing within these areas, well, I base this not so much on my personal taste but on what I believe are the three things that anthologies should do. First, I believe an anthology should be about discovery. It should introduce writers to new audiences; and, conversely, it should introduce audiences to emerging and established writers whose work deserves further amplification. Second, I believe that an anthology should offer insight into the craft of writing. That is to say, it should offer a close-up on style and form and the different ways in which themes are developed by writers. Finally, I believe that an anthology should always offer fresh perspectives and insights. The kind that illuminates current cultural moments and shed light on important points from the past.

—Said (Amir Said),
Paris, France
January 3, 2019

Introduction

You will find few people in the past 20 years that have been as committed as Dart Adams has been to the study, discussion, and lively debate of hip hop culture. One of the most recognized names in hip hop writing today, Dart is a non-conformist who has butted heads against more than one member of hip hop journalism's established brands. In such instances, an objective observer might have said that Dart would have done better for himself by simply going along with the pack and not making any waves. But Dart is…Dart, which means he stands his ground — no matter what side of the debate he's on — and he will call foul on something or someone whenever he sees it.

This does not mean that Dart is your garden variety contrarian trolling his way to Twitter fame. On the contrary, Dart is very well informed about the history of hip hop culture, and he genuinely takes ill-informed write-ups, think pieces, and tweets as personal affront to the culture he knows and loves. In this vein, Dart does not beg to be deemed an authority on the culture — though he has earned that description; nor does whine or complain about the obvious blackballing from some hip hop publications that he's had to endure. Dart soldiers on. He doesn't waiver in his commitment to research or his dedication to documenting the culture in the best way that he can. So his hip hop bonafides aside, there's also something refreshing and noble about a guy who refuses to play the game and stands firm on what he believes in.

Above it all, what stands out the most about Dart for me, and I trust that readers of this single-author edition of *Best Damn Hip Hop Writing* will agree, is that his work reflects the knowledge of someone who's spent considerable time dissecting key developments in and important aspects of hip hop culture. Dart's work is never rare on insight; and his focus on hip hop's history is particularly valuable for younger generations who want to gain a better understanding of all of the nuance of by-gone eras of the '80s and '90s. Collectively, *Best Damn Hip Hop Writing: The Book of Dart* represents the work of a veteran writer who, in many ways, is only just beginning.

—Said (Amir Said),
Paris, France
March 21, 2019

Part 1
CRITICAL
OBSERVATIONS

Hip Hop Has Always Been an Inclusive Art Form and an Exclusive Culture; Mainstream Rap Music Isn't: A Rebuttal to Yoh's Article "Hip-Hop Needs to Be an Inclusive Artform— Not an Exclusive Culture"

Early in 2018, Yoh (senior writer at DJ Booth) wrote an op-ed which quoted a line from a piece I was commissioned to write for NPR commemorating the 40th anniversary of the inception of hip hop culture, as well as a tweet from Freddie Foxxx stating the need for hip hop to once again be exclusive. Yoh, 26, added the disclosure that he never experienced any of the previous eras when hip hop culture and rap weren't already mainstream fixtures, and he emphasized that his perspective was shaped by growing up in a post-Telecom Act/post-rap apartheid world where two separate and unequal rap industries co-existed simultaneously.

Since Yoh never saw the events unfold in real time, nor did he witness the fallout over a full calendar year afterward, he's only known the rap scene as a thriving environment. Like many younger hip hop fans who are currently under the age of 40, Yoh made the understandable mistake of conflating rap, the rap industry, and all of its corporate byproducts as being included under the umbrella of "hip hop." They aren't.

When Freddie Foxxx was talking about making hip hop exclusive again, I understood exactly where he was coming from. Hip hop culture and rap music possess a unique space in the continuum of black American music due to several odd factors.

First, early black music forms such as gospel, blues, jazz, doo-wop, soul/R&B, and rock 'n' roll relied on someone with white-skin privilege in order to get financed, recorded, distributed, and/or get radio airplay. This was due to racism, economics, and a lack of access. In turn, this led to a cycle of exploitation and inequality, which stemmed from a lack of ownership. Not only were these black artists often stripped of their own creations and intellectual property, but it also meant that they couldn't receive any royalties or future compensation for their own innovations or pioneering. It did, however, make the children of label owners that signed these acts to recording deals rich, since they owned the rights to their back catalogs. Cue the theme song to "The Neverending Story"...

In the case of rap music, there were several black-owned record labels that sought to benefit from the Bronx's burgeoning hip hop culture by recording the first big rap hit. Both Sylvia Robinson of Sugar Hill Records and Bobby Robinson of Enjoy Records saw the potential of rap music early on, but rather than sign up an elite hip hop crew, they scouted and gathered information on all the leading crews — and the scene as a whole — to better determine how to gain an advantage. They soon realized that the DJ — not the rappers — was the focal point of the hip hop crew, and they sought to exploit that appeal.

The rappers would audition for the DJ in order to be in the crew, and oftentimes after being paid, rappers were encouraged to kick back some of the money to help maintain the sound system and purchase better equipment. Both Sugar Hill and Enjoy sought out rappers and offered them, at one time, approximately 25- to 50-shows worth of pay to sign. They were then told they didn't need to split the pot with the DJ. Also, they'd record over a musical track created by a live band. So the DJ — the very backbone of hip hop culture — wasn't necessary. From its inception back in 1979 to today, the rap music industry has NEVER been "pure."

While early hip hop crews and rap artists were being exploited, taken advantage of, and suppressed by black-owned labels like Sugar Hill, Enjoy, and Winley, to make matters worse, rap wasn't even regarded as "real" music by the black music community at large. Black radio programmers mostly abhorred rap; at best, they tolerated it. Even crucial black music advocates and gatekeepers like Frankie Crocker and Don Cornelius were resistant. Major labels eventually began to record rap acts — Tommy Boy, Profile, Jive/Zomba — but they were few and far between. In time, Def Jam would set forth the blueprint for the fortification of a rap label, thanks in large part to label co-founder Russell Simmons, who also owned Rush Artist Management, which oversaw the careers of rap's biggest draws at the time. This is the kind of early ownership that no other form or subgenre of black music had previously enjoyed.

Critically, it helped that rap was also directly attached to hip hop culture. There's a passage in Yoh's article where he writes, "The hip-hop I know has saved the lives of all creeds and brought joy to every color. Exclusive art doesn't change, help, or save lives." The hip hop culture I know of has done the very same. — From the very beginning it changed, helped and saved lives, including my own—; but only when it was a subculture far away from the prying eyes of the mainstream, Madison Avenue, or Hollywood.

Hip hop was inclusive from the outset. Everyone brought influences from their ethnic backgrounds, countries of origin, neighborhoods, and their own individuality into their chosen means of self-expression within hip hop. Although there were few early on, white kids were among the legendary graffiti writers, b-boys and eventually even rappers and DJs alongside their black and Latino peers. White folks such as Henry Chalfant, Marty Cooper, Charlie Ahearn, Debbie Harry, Chris Stein, Tom Silverman, Arthur Baker, Bill Adler, Rick Rubin, Lyor Cohen, Ruza Blue, and Sal Abbetiello, among others, were heavily involved in bringing local, national and then global attention to hip hop culture, helping it to spread like a wildfire. Even noted culture vultures, like Malcolm McLaren, were allowed entrance in before the novelty wore off and the next trend to capitalize on became their priority.

Hip hop also incorporated its travels into the Downtown scene, the modern art world, and punk influences with little to no problem. At no point was hip hop/rap something you had to seek out, put in real effort to participate in, or log serious man-hours for in order to gain acceptance. Hip hop's "exclusive feel" back then was never a deterrent to anyone who wanted to be a part of it.

Though no fault of his own, Yoh didn't experience the stretches between 1981-84, 1986-89, or 1990-92, where rap — , and by extension hip hop culture, — made inroads and breakthroughs to the mainstream. There was a time when, in order to be a rap fan, you were also by extension a supporter, participant, or contributor to hip hop culture as a whole. With the passage of time, rap became removed from the wider culture that had birthed it, which has removed the need for participants and fans alike to learn its history or study it; unlike other art forms or disciplines where such an education would be required.

The staple breakbeats and records rappers and b-boys employed were from every musical genre imaginable. The artistic influences and references found in aerosol art on trains spanned from classic comic strips, to cartoons and comic books to contemporary art found in galleries. B-boys drew inspiration and incorporated moves from kung-fu films, the salsa and merengue they danced to at home, as well as old film footage of tap dancers or whatever dance moves they saw in film or television.

The point is that hip hop's inclusivity was always one of its strengths. However, those within hip hop had to learn and study their craft and respect the culture as they were the ones contributing to it. There was a built-in apprenticeship program with checks and balances installed in every single cultural discipline. With those who solely look to profit from the genre, that's never been a concern.

"I only know hip hop as a massive entity. An inclusive, embracive culture of many doors for easy entry. Before my time there were rules to participation that have vanished — now almost anyone with a functioning microphone can place their art underneath her umbrella," Yoh wrote. This is part of the problem with rap now. Whereas before there were barriers to entry for an artist, a process he or she had to follow just to become nice enough to be considered ready to enter a studio and record a song, in the era of home studios, email, and Pro Tools, anything goes. With the passage of time, coupled with advances in both production and communications technologies, this has only gotten worse.

Once an artist could record his or her own music on a laptop and upload it to their SoundClick page and then sell it on their MySpace's SnoCap store, there was no chance rap's Pandora's Box would ever be closed. Based on the previous continuum, between 1979 and 1997, we should've had at least two more golden eras in rap, but there hasn't been one since, thanks to major record labels scaling back A&R departments, outsourcing artist development, and furthering the mainstream-underground industry divide.

Hip hop has always been inclusive. If you spoke another language? Incorporate that into your music. If you came from a unique background? Rap about it or reference it in your art/music/production. Play an instrument? Do it. Can you sing? Find a way to work that into your output, too. Hip hop, much like the hybrid martial arts philosophy Jeet Kune Do, stresses expressing yourself honestly through your art and being original so that you could gain acceptance on your own terms rather than by copying others. However, rap was also about influence, inspiration, and competition that led to innovation, style evolutions, and the overall growth of the genre.

What Yoh recognizes as the "hip hop" he loves and grew up with is to older cats like myself a watered down corporate byproduct far removed from the hip hop we grew up listening to. The hip hop WE grew up with was only played at night, hated by our elders, located all the way at the back of the record store, and it didn't even have serious publications dedicated to it until well over a decade into its existence. But it was always an inclusive art form.

Hip Hop's Ever Growing Generation Chasm

On January 15, 2014, the news came that Pete DJ Jones, one of the unsung pioneers of hip hop culture, passed away. Pete DJ Jones was a Bronx club DJ that not only is credited with being the first DJ to play the same record on two turntables in order to extend the song but he's also reported to have had presented the first emcee in rap history, even before Kool Herc introduced Coke La Rock on the mic sometime between 1973 and 1974. Kool Herc, Afrika Bambaataa and Pete DJ Jones often had soundclashes in the Bronx during the early days of the burgeoning hip hop movement. Jones was older than both Herc and Bambaataa, so he attracted and played for a slightly different audience, but he was still instrumental in helping to spread the culture to neighboring boroughs before it ultimately went nationwide in 1979, and then global between 1983 and 1984.

Since hip hop was a youth culture, that meant that many of the early graffiti writers, B-boys, DJ's and emcees had relatively short careers. A lot of the early legends essentially aged out of their respective disciplines. However, hip hop culture had a built in mentorship/apprentice program so the previous generation would teach and prepare the following generation of who would then add their own style of evolutions; and they would in turn pass on their knowledge to a new generation that would do the same. This is essentially how the culture worked between 1973 and 1984. But then the outside world (read: corporate world) became interested in hip hop.

By 1985, media oversaturation forced B-boys underground, thus removing one of hip hop culture's elements from us. B-boying relied on the older cats teaching to the youth about finding & and developing their one styles to express themselves. In addition, it taught them how to dance to the record and accentuate it, as opposed to doing power moves or acrobatics to wow an audience. With that key mentorship link to the younger generation removed, hip hop culture was left with graffiti writing, DJ'ing and emceeing on the slate.

Even though graf writing was the first of the four elements in existence and the first one to attract any media coverage, it's been saved by the fact that it's an outlaw culture and is illegal. This means that it's extremely tough for corporate interests to infiltrate it enough to change its actual culture. But it's still susceptible to being exploited and used for commercial means. The de facto mentorship program that's existed with graffiti is still alive and well after more than 45 years. Younger graf writers have been tracing older graf writers' outlines and practicing hand styles, control, and spraying techniques for close to 40 years. Older DJ's would mentor younger DJ's and sometimes these younger DJ's would introduce or discover style evolutions which ultimately forced the previous generation to fall back. This was true with both Grandmaster Flash & and Grand Wizard Theodore, who both ended up taking the audiences of their idols, mentors, and even their own family members due to their technical brilliance and showmanship behind the wheels of steel. Same was true in rap where the old school emcees that rocked the park jams, school gyms, CYO's, PAL's, and even the clubs would meet their match at the hands of younger, more dynamic and lyrical emcees. The New School emcees eventually eclipsed the Old School emcees. It was essentially like Darwin's Theory Of Evolution meets a Shaw Brothers Kung Fu film.

Rap music is an urban music form that started out as a youth culture. As I go forward in explaining how the current generational chasm in Rap music occurred, it's imperative that you keep this in mind. Young people typically develop their sense of taste or preferences in music, art, and film or and begin to assert their individuality between the ages of 9 and 14. Incidentally, in urban music, a new generation or wave happens every 3 to 5 years. Black music became album based between 1967 and 1968. This is around the same time that graffiti first spread throughout New York City.

It took from the summer of 1973, when hip hop culture had its beginnings in the Bronx, NY, to fall of 1979 before rap music went national; thanks to a the record label Sugar Hill Records. By 1984, Rap had gone mainstream thanks to several Hollywood films and the success of Run-DMC'S debut album, Run-DMC. Between rap's introduction and it going mainstream, in that 5-year span there were two distinct rap generations split into two factions: the Old School and New School. It is here where we begin to explore the phenomenon of the generation gap in regards to rap music.

The Old Schoolers, who came up performing at block parties, jams, school gyms, and then moved up to clubs, resented those New Schoolers who recorded and made LP's. The Old Schoolers, who mostly never got the same opportunities to record albums, felt that the New Schoolers hadn't paid their dues. They especially resented the fact that New Schoolers were eclipsing their popularity, despite the fact that they hadn't spent years honing their craft in the same fashion that the Old Schoolers had done. In turn, you had a generation of kids that were the new rap audience. This new rap audience didn't remember a time before records, a time when one had to rely strictly on secondhand audio cassette tapes from park jams. To this new rap audience, the so-called "New School" and "Old School" was indistinguishable. They just preferred some rap groups and emcees to others for various reasons.

Every 3 to 5 years, rap had these new "generations" that forced many rappers and groups to tap out because they couldn't compete with the new breed of rappers, and producers or adapt to the new rap terrain following the newest innovations, technologies, techniques or style evolutions. Back when rap and hip hop were still very much considered "youth culture," it made sense that teenagers were capable of making classics so the young lions could actually best the old lions and usurp them. It isn't much different from when the new skateboarding tricks sprung up in the mid- to late '80s that forced several previous generations of pro skateboarders out of competitions that weren't capable of frequently landing them.

Let's revisit an earlier point. If you typically begin paying real attention to music between the ages of 9 to 14, this is also probably around the time that you began your personal journey as a rap fan. If you started early (bonus points if you have older siblings that aged you up and you began paying attention sooner), that exposed you to more and more generations of rappers and producers. The next key component in the present rap generation chasm occurred between 25 and 30 years ago. It's commonly referred to as the "Golden Era". Some people believe it that the Golden Era was one continuous period that stretched from 1986 to 1996. Others (myself included) maintain that it was two separate eras, with one transition period in between. The first Golden Era lasting from 1986 to 1989, and the second Golden Era spanning from 1992 to 1996. All of the keys to understanding the widening generation gap in rap music can be found by studying this period.

The main reason why the Golden Eras are key to understanding the present day generation chasm is because the widely accepted aesthetics for what constitutes "classic hip hop/rap" were all established between the years 1986 and 1996. The so-called "hip hop/rap purists" cling to this era, and many of them dismiss any rap that doesn't follow a similar formula or sound comparable as garbage. This is where the first solid lines in the sand in regards to the many generations of rap fans are drawn.

Why is this era the one where this happened? The reasons are numerous, but the perfect-storm combination of recording and music production technologies, new production innovations and techniques, lyrical style evolutions, and the fiercest level of competition — coupled with Rap music becoming album centric between 1987 and 1988 — all led to the explosion called the "Golden Era". Most rappers or and producers who are widely regarded as legends today either survived this era, thrived in it or were heavily influenced by it. Keep in mind that when I say "Golden Era," I'm referring to the extended period between 1986 to 1996, which includes two Golden Eras.

During this span of time, which lasted more than a decade, there was time for two or three new generations of rap fans to either enter the fray or lose interest in it altogether. If you consider all of the benchmarks and classic recordings that were made between 1986 and 1996, it's no surprise why those who experienced this era or grew up during it would advocate so fiercely for it. To them, everything in the rap world seemingly changed overnight. Beginning in 1997, the aesthetics of rap transformed and a new era dawned; an era that is often referred to as the Jiggy Era. It was a complete departure from the previous decade of rap, and it would set into the motion the second half of the process that created today's generation gap in rap: the eventual separation between the mainstream and underground rap worlds.

As I've stated before, hip hop culture had a built-in mentorship program. Typically, the older cats would mentor the youth and they'd pass them the torch or they'd just force them out of the game for one reason or another. In regards to rap listeners, they were either introduced to rap by an older sibling or relative. This was how it pretty much went from 1979 to 1996 (although there was a stretch of upheaval during the transition period between the two Golden Eras where a mini generation gap occurred, but that's another story). In 1997, a new rift began the opening that has become the current generational chasm. Again, hip hop culture had its own built-in mentorship program and it was the underground that helped to provide much of the checks and balances necessary for the art form's growth. Without the underground, there would've been no first Golden Era and there certainly wouldn't have been a second. However, fallout resulting from the signing of the Telecommunications Act Of 1996 aided in the eventual state of hip hop Apartheid that exists today. Two rap industries existing at the same time, both separate and unequal.

When the radio stopped playing certain artists that were once popular, and when the overall sound and aesthetic of rap music began changing, listeners who remember how things were during the Golden Era(s), or even before, took a pronounced step back. Many went with the underground, as it still upheld what they believed to be the desired sound and feel of rap music, which harkened back to the Golden Era(s). Some older music heads just became disinterested altogether and focused on other genres of music like Electronica. What about the new listeners and the younger fans whose introduction to rap was the Jiggy Era? Well...

During this period between 1997 and 1999, an odd phenomenon occurred where there was a clear splintering within distinct generations of rap listeners. Those that were old enough to remember the entirety of the second Golden Era didn't much care for the Jiggy Era. But those slightly younger, who had only caught the tail end of it, were split. And those even younger than them had no clue that any drastic change had even occurred. It was the music on the radio and all over the Viacom networks, so it was just the rap that was popular at the time. Nothing more, nothing less.

While in previous years (with the exception of the aforementioned transitional period between Golden Eras) older siblings would influence the rap their younger siblings listened to, this odd change occurred where the older sibling retreated underground or delved into R&B or electronica, leaving their younger sibling (and their entire peer group) to their own devices. This was the generation of rap listeners who had never owned cassette tapes and had only owned CD's. This was the same generation of rap listeners that grew up with the internet, as opposed those adults who did not experience the internet as children. In fact, the internet was the tool that helped to widen this generation gap in rap. As the speed of communications technology became progressively faster, the generation gap between rap fans ultimately grew into a chasm.

Several independent rap albums in 1997 denoted the beginning of a divergent era for Rap music. These included Latryx: The Album by Lateef & Lyrics Born, Funcrusher Plus by Company Flow, Overcast! by Atmosphere, and Soundbombing, a compilation the by Rawkus Records. These albums simply didn't appeal to younger rap fans, but there was an older crowd, especially college-aged, which gravitated to rap along these lines. Those who preferred the mainstream rap that was gaining favor all but eschewed underground rap, and soon it was remanded to indie labels. An older brother would play Company Flow in his headphones, while the younger brother played DMX in his. As time passed, they would share fewer and fewer of the same favorites rappers, groups, or producers. One of the earliest indicators of this generational gap is how many younger rap fans regard Nas's It Was Written as being as good as his classic debut Illmatic. Older rap listeners maintain that It Was Written was is an obvious step down quality wise. That's just the tip of the iceberg…

Why is the rap generation chasm such a big deal? Well, for one let's think about "classic" albums and how it has affected them. Consider all the Rap albums that were released that are across the board revered as "classic" albums Between 1997 and 2003. There are a significant number of indie rap albums that don't get the same distinction only because mainstream rap listeners never heard them. You might wonder why that's weird considering indie albums don't sell a great deal of units? But the fact is, most of the albums from the Golden Era(s) that are universally accepted as classics didn't sell very well at all. The difference is there wasn't a split that occurred which affected the way these albums were processed by rap fans.

This becomes a larger issue every year following 2004, where the profile and embrace of indie and underground rap albums decreases dramatically. Thus, the generation chasm prevents these indie and underground rap albums from being regarded as "classic" material simply because no more universal agreements can be made about what constitutes a "classic" album anymore.

This issue often rears its ugly head when rap journalists, who are largely comprised of the post-mainstream/underground-split era, are asked to write classic-album lists or list classic songs. Since these multiple generations of rap listeners weren't exposed to the full palate of rap music, their knowledge of rap often only going back as far as 1997, they have a limited knowledge base to draw from. This is how Cam'ron's Purple Haze ends up often being viewed as a classic by these journalists while an album like Madvillain's Madvillainy is not. (Actually, this is the same reason why so many deserving indie and underground releases end up missing from rap albums lists.)

Let's finish this off by returning to my point about how rap is still viewed as being a part of a "youth culture". One of the key issues rap is having at the moment, besides it being at it's all time low point both creatively and lyrically at the mainstream level, is that many of the top rappers have been in the game in excess of a decade. In the early days of rap, having a 10-year career was astonishing. Now Jay-Z and Nas, for instance, have been around since the early '90s, and several other rappers who are still relevant are holdovers from previous eras. When the biggest star in all of rap music is 44 years old, and the genre recorded version of the form for 35 years, at some point it ceases being a "youth culture".

When rap was the dominion of young, hungry, inventive emcees that would push the boundaries of the art form to the point where the previous generation had to hand over the reins, it was different. Today, emcees like Black Thought , who has a careers spanning two decades, can still dispatch any young lions in the game.

This resentment from the younger cats that can't take the game over adds to the generation gap. What we're currently left with is a huge chasm akin to the Grand Canyon in width and depth. The fact is, the new waves of emcees can't force the old ones out of the game anymore. This puts rap into a new space that it's never experienced before. And my generation, the one that retreated to the underground like the Morlocks from the "X-Men" comic books, is in large part to blame for this generation chasm. We're the ones who broke away and didn't do for the youth what the older kids did for us. We let our little brothers, sisters and cousins gleefully recite "Bling Bling" while retreated to our headphones and played Common & Sadat X's 1999 to combat it rather than actively bridging the gap. Now I'm just left sitting in front of a MacBook wondering "What if?"

1981: The Year Hip Hop Broke

As far as the nascent musical form of rap was concerned, 1981 was a year like none other. first appeared on record in the Summer of 1979, and by early1980 it had its first Billboard hits in early 1980, and it continued to grow in popularity all throughout the year. By January 1981, Blondie had released "Rapture," the 2nd second single from their album Automaerican (1980), which featured Debbie Harry rhyming and namedropping a couple of hip hop's luminaries in a rhyme such as FAB 5 FREDDY and the even then legendary DJ Grandmaster Flash. "Rapture" was tucked away as the second song on Side B of Autoamerican and there wasn't much indication that it was going to become a single. And certainly there was no indication that it would eclipse the popularity of their previous smash hit single, the Reggae/Ska-tinged "Tide Is High."

"Rapture" was officially released on January 12, 1981, but it really didn't take off until after the music video for it debuted on the television show "Solid Gold" on January 31, 1981. The song steadily gained more and more traction on radio and then swiftly ascended the Billboard charts as the weeks passed. Then Blondie was invited to be the musical guests on the late night network sketch comedy show "Saturday Night Live" in February, so they consulted with their friends for a hot rap act to bring out with them to on "Saturday Night Live."

It was February 14 — Valentine's Day — 1981 when Debbie Harry and Chris Stein of Blondie sprang a surprise on the studio audience by allowing Funky 4 +1 to perform a set. This was a huge opportunity for Funk 4 +1; but more importantly, it was also the first time a rap group performed live on national television, complete with an actual DJ as opposed to a live band. Once they rocked the house, things began to snowball from there for rap on the national stage. "Rapture" became a huge success. It wasn't just a radio smash and a club sensation, it was also a go-to jam for DJ's and a guaranteed floor filler at the block party. It "Rapture" eventually reached the #1 spot on the Billboard Hot 100 and held it for two consecutive weeks (from March 28 to April 4); it also reached Top 5 in the UK. For many people, "Rapture" represented the first time that they'd ever heard rap music. The new interest and curiosity in rap ultimately led to the release of many new rap records between the spring and summer of 1981. Labels like Sugar Hill, Enjoy, Winley, Spring, West End, Tay-Ster, Tommy Boy, and Profile were put out rap singles at a furious rate.

The April 22, 1981 edition of Village Voice featured the Sally Banes and Martha Cooper article "Physical Graffiti: Breaking Is Hard To Do," which became the first published piece to center B-Boys and B-Boy culture. The article was more than a year in the making, In January 1980, Martha Cooper encountered a group of young B-Boys as they were being arrested by the police. The boys maintained that they were only "rocking". Cooper convinced them to show her what they were doing, and when the youth began to dance she instinctively began taking pictures.

Martha Cooper contacted her friend Sally Banes and they attempted to track down those B-Boys. Cooper and Banes learned that those boys had quit, but their search eventually lead them to discover — through Henry Chalfant, a fellow photographer who also took pictures of subway graffiti — a crew of active B-Boys. Cooper and Banes interviewed B-Boys and observed several practices and performances at Common Ground, a converted loft in SoHo which doubled as an exhibition space for art and photos as well as a practice space for B-Boys. The combination of Banes's descriptive prose and Cooper's amazing photos really captured the attention of readers. A follow up article in the May

15th, 1981 Friday edition of The New York Times announced a series of public B-Boy exhibitions would take place at New York University during The Bronx Folklore Conference on May 16 and 17, 1981. It was here that many people outside of hip hop culture got their first exposure to both B-Boying and the Rock Steady Crew, the crew that would eventually become the most infamous B-Boy crew of all time.

Another oft-overlooked incident from 1981 that further helped to spread rap to a mainstream audience came courtesy of a highly unlikely source: comedian Mel Brooks. On June 12, 1981 his film History Of The World, Part 1 was released. The film featured the song "It's Good To Be The King." It was a rap that he recorded to promote the film. While it was largely viewed as a novelty song, it still managed to become a minor hit. Sylvia Robinson (owner of Sugar Hill Records) refusing to be outdone recorded her own version called "It's Good To Be The Queen." Between the growing popularity of rap and the groundswell of interest in B-Boying (or "breaking" as it was called by 1984) it was only a matter of time before a news feature was forthcoming.

In July 1981 (the exact airdate cannot be determined but it's believed to have been early on in the month), ABC aired a special report on their then popular show "20/20" titled "Rappin' To The Beat" by Steve Fox. This special report featured Kurtis Blow, Funky 4+1, Sugar Hill Gang, and The Furious 5, and the Rock Steady Crew, with commentary from Debbie Harry of Blondie, legendary radio personality Jocko Henderson, and a clip of punk band The Clash performing rap-inspired selections from their groundbreaking 1980 LP Sandinista!. This "20/20" segment inspired several people at home to rap and legions of youth became B-Boys overnight.

On the graffiti front, 1981 was the year the medium — which was once relegated to walls, bridges, trains, and the outside and inside of subway cars — entered art galleries via canvases. (A decade earlier, in July 1971, the first ever article about graffiti ran in The New York Times titled "TAKI 183 Spawns Pen Pals.") In October, 1980, renowned graffiti artist CRASH's "GAS" show at Fashion Moda in SoHo led to an explosion of graffiti art shows in galleries beginning with the New York/New Wave exhibition in Queens' PS 1 in February 1981. It became such a success that it led to numerous other art events at galleries and venues all over New York City, such as Fun Gallery, Grafitti Above Ground, Mudd Club, 51X, and even the Kenny Gallery in Manhattan's Art & Design High School. 1981 is also largely considered the year that the entire East Village scene exploded and numerous graffiti writers made their first inroads into the burgeoning New York art scene (a snowball effect following the success of the "Beyond Words" art show at the Mudd Club in April 1981). At this same time, hip hop began its trek from the venues of the South Bronx and to the top spots Downtown.

The Rock Steady Crew had already made its way from SoHo's Common Ground and The Kitchen to performing in clubs like The Ritz, Mudd Club, and Negril. Michael Holman's Negril parties first popped off in October 1981, around the same time Rock Steady performed their highly influential "Graffiti Rock" shows at The Kitchen, with which featured FAB 5 FREDDY as the host and art from top graffiti artists LEE and DONDI. During this time, Afrika Bambataa had begun DJ'ing in Downtown clubs and Zulu Nation members, B-Boys, and hip hop fans began to interact with Punk and New Wave crowds. This resulted in things like Malcolm McLaren working with The World Famous Supreme Team, overseas tours, and rap groups opening for The Clash in the near future.

By the close of 1981, Rock Steady Crew was drawing large audiences for exhibitions, like the legendary Lincoln Center battle vs. Dynamic Rockers in August 1981. RSC was also faced with battling crews who took to B-Boying either after having read about them in the Village Voice, saw them on "20/20," caught them rocking at a live demo around the city, or battling another rival crew. Rap continued to gain traction to the point that FAB 5 FREDDY had proposed the idea to filmmaker Charlie Ahearn that they should make a film about the intersecting worlds of DJ'ing, graffiti, B-Boying, and emceeing. The initial concept would eventually be fully fleshed out and become the feature film Wild Style.

All the while, the Downtown art scene was exploding thanks in part to the new blood infused by all the graffiti artists having shows in East Village galleries and rubbing shoulders with art world darlings like Jean Michel Basquiat and Keith Haring. They swiftly went from outsiders to contemporaries and peers. Suddenly, they all were getting coverage in publications such as Artforum, Art In America, Art Monthly (UK) and ARTnews. Artists like CRASH, FUTURA, DONDI, LEE, STASH, DAZE, and ZEPHYR became "legitimate" and earned money selling canvases and original pieces to collectors both stateside and overseas, since graffiti had also become the new hot thing in the art world in Europe in 1981.

While Charlie Ahearn and FAB 5 FREDDY were planning to do their first round of shooting at the Dixie Club in The Bronx that October for their film Wild Style, filming had already begun on Henry Chalfant's hip hop documentary Style Wars in June 1981. The battle between Rock Steady Crew vs. and Dynamic Rockers seen in the film took place at United Skates Of America in Queens. That same month, Rock Steady Crew's "20/20" segment was shot, and Rock Steady Crew ended up playing prominent roles in both films Wild Style and Style Wars.

Both Wild Style and Style Wars wouldn't be completed until 1983. By comparison, Downtown '81, Edo Bertoglio and Glenn O'Brien's film that catalogued New York's Downtown art scene starring Jean Michel Basquiat, which was filmed in the

East Village and Lower East Side between December 1980 and January 1981, didn't see a proper release until the 2000 Cannes Film Festival. Debbie Harry of Blondie, FAB 5 FREDDY, and LEE all make cameo appearances in Downtown '81 to further cement how their worlds all intertwined.

1982 technically marks the year that hip hop was mentioned in print. The first print article to mention hip hop culture by name was written by Michael Holman in 1981 and published in the East Village Eye magazine in January 1982, when Holman interviewed Afrika Bambaataa. But this January, 1982 date doesn't change the fact hip hop's individual elements had all broken nationally and/or received their first mainstream exposure in 1981. Not only that, but the films that are widely credited with presenting all of the elements of hip hop culture under one umbrella both began filming in 1981, following the first ever national news segment that showcased the connection between rap and B-Boying.

By 1984, Hollywood had robbed not only the premises and storylines of both Wild Style and Style Wars for the first wave of "hip hop" themed films, but they even plundered Martha Cooper's first encounter with B-Boys. They'd already totally removed Martha from the equation when it was recounted by a police officer for the aforementioned 1981 "20/20" segment. This factual encounter between B-Boys and the police was plundered and further dramatized in the film Beat Street. By the time the films Breakin' and Beat Street were in theaters, most people had no access to either Wild Style or Style Wars, and even fewer had the wherewithal to document what was happening, as just 5 years previous rap was summarily dismissed as a fad across the board.

In 1981, I was only in the 1st grade, but I was reading record labels from the collection of my upstairs neighbors' sons who were both DJ's. I remember being shocked seeing Benny Hill rapping on my television one night on PBS. And I'll never forget that "20/20" feature on ABC because I saw Rock Steady Crew and Kurtis

Blow on my television at a time rap didn't appear on television or in mainstream publications. The day after that "20/20" special report, there were kids trying their damndest to replicate what they saw in the play area of the Blackstone School in the South End/Lower Roxbury. Shortly afterwards, we encountered the Floorlords, Boston's longest running B-Boy crew who introduced us to the basics and fundamentals of B-Boying.

Hard to imagine that more than 35 years ago, hip hop culture was first being exposed to a wider audience through a novelty song, the filming of a national news story, and the first scenes shot for a documentary. In the immortal words of the late, great Christopher Wallace, "I never thought hip hop would take it this far."

1990:
Rap's Forgotten Transition Year

1990 represented the end of Rap's first Golden Era and the alpha of the process of building towards yet another one...

There has been a long raging debate amongst rap scholars and hip hop aficionados about whether or not there was one continuous Golden Era lasting from 1986 to 1996 and whether there were actually two separate periods with a transition period between them or just one. If there was a first Golden Era, when did it begin, and why and when did it end? In this essay, I'm going to deconstruct the transition year of 1990 and provide all the context necessary to make it clear that one Golden Era came to a close while building towards another one.

The new direction urban music took in 1990 actually had its origins in late 1989 with the rise of international club music. The floodgates first opened up after German producer Frank Farian hit it big when he capitalized on Milli Vanilli's first two 1988 hit singles ("Girl You Know It's True" and "Baby Don't Forget My Number"). In March 1989, Milli Vanilli's album Girl You Know It's True was released, and it shot up the charts immediately. By January 1990, it had 3 #1 singles, "Baby Don't Forget My Number," "Blame It On The Rain," and "Girl I'm Gonna Miss You". The album peaked at #2 and sold 6 million copies in the United States alone. The male duo that comprised Milli Vanillli were later discovered to be frauds. Essentially, they were lip-sync singers with the right look to front the sound. Their fraud notwithstanding, the uptempo, dance-oriented club sound that Milli Vanilli had helped to popularize found a rabid following.

March 1989 also marked the same month that the UK's Soul II Soul's released their lead single "Keep On Movin'." Their album Club Classics Vol. One (called Keep On Movin' in the United States) was released in the following April and it went double Platinum, powered by the hit singles "Keep On Movin'" and "Back To Life (However Do You Want Me)." International dance/club music made huge inroads throughout the tail end of 1989, thereby changing the aesthetic of not only urban music but slowly shifting the sound of what passed for mainstream hits. Throughout 1989, rap hits like Tone Loc's "Wild Thing", Young MC's "Bust A Move," and De La Soul's "Me, Myself & I" all did extremely well on the Hot 100 Billboard charts, as well as hitting #1 on the R&B/Rap charts.

Throughout 1989, MTV's hit show "Club MTV" became increasingly popular. It initially focused on freestyle and house music acts, (like Information Society, Sweet Sensation, The Cover Girls, Exposé, Seduction, Inner City, Ten City, etc.) But as international club music gained more favor, Milli Vanilli, Soul II Soul, Cathy Dennis, D Mob, and Technotronic closed out the year strong. In 1990, that sound would explode and pretty much take over both the urban and Pop music worlds.

It all began in September 1989 with the North American release of Belgian dance music team Technotronic's initial single "Pump Up The Jam." In November 1989, Salt N' Pepa released their lead single "Expression". Both "Pump Up The Jam" and "Expression" climbed up the charts that November. In the first week of January 1990, saw the German outfit Snap! dropped what would become their big-hit single: "The Power". The following week, Technotronic's dropped "Get Up! (Before The Night Is Over)", follow-up single to "Pump Up The Jam." Just one week later, MC Hammer released "U Can't Touch This," the song that would be the catalyst that would forever changed the rap music landscape.

After "U Can't Touch This," nothing in rap would ever be the same again. MC Hammer won American Music Awards (1990)

in two of the three rap categories for his 1989 album Let's Get
It Started. He won over Tone Loc and Eazy E both times that
year, and he led off the "U Can't Touch This" video with the
American Music Awards footage, as if to further cement the
song's bragadocious claim.

As all of these aforementioned songs dominated the radio and
their videos entered the regular rotation on MTV, Salt N' Pepa's
"Expression" began to gain more and more traction. On January
20th, 1990 it knocked The D.O.C's "The D.O.C. & The Doctor"
out of the top spot on the Billboard rap charts after a 2-week
stay. "Expression" would enjoy an 8-week run on the top of the
Billboard Rap charts from January 20th to March 10th, 1990. It
was finally dethroned by Digital Underground's "The Humpty
Dance," which would go on to occupy that same position for the
next 5 weeks straight.

"The D.O.C. & The Doctor" was a hard, boom bap, lyrical
rap song, while both "Expression" and "The Humpty Dance,"
both more dance and club inspired than boom bap lyrical, not
only dominated the rap charts but both singles went Platinum.
"Expression" peaked at #28 on the Billboard Hot 100 but "The
Humpty Dance" made it up all the way to #11. It was clear to
anyone that was paying attention: 1990 was going to be the year
that a rap song was finally going to capture the #1 spot on the
Billboard Hot 100. It was just a matter of who'd accomplish it
first. Rappers and producers had finally cracked the code of how to
consistently make crossover rap. All that was left was the inevitable
fallout, jealously, and backlash.

In 1990, there were several more developments that occurred
that changed the urban music terrain. In late February 1990, Bell
Biv Devoe released "Poison," a raunchy R&B song with a rap beat
that also resonated with the pop audience and clubgoers. "Poison"
worked on radio, and in the club. It was always heard blasting
out of jeeps. And its video got constant burn on both MTV and

BET. It was a song that could be played on MTV's "Club MTV" and "Yo! MTV Raps," as well as BET's "Video Soul" and "Video Vibrations." Its steady ascent up multiple charts was emblematic of a sea change happening in the world of music in 1990.

The international club music's stranglehold on the music scene of 1990 was bolstered by the release of Italian house music production team Black Box's single "Everybody Everybody" in March 1990. The track would eventually hit #1 on the Hot Dance Club Play charts; it peaked at #2 on the R&B/Rap charts and #8 on the Billboard Hot 100. The album "Dreamland" would be released in May 1990, reach Gold sales and produce one more hit single ("Strike It Up") which also peaked at #8 on Billboard's Hot 100.

The success of pop-leaning rap or rap songs that happened to cross over, like Salt N' Pepa's "Expression", MC Hammer's "U Can't Touch This", Digital Underground's "The Humpty Dance", Snap!'s "The Power", Kid N' Play's "Funhouse," Mellow Man Ace's "Mentirosa," along with the runaway platinum sales of Bell Biv Devoe's "Poison," changed the way some rappers approached making music. And it made some record labels encourage — if not force — their artists force or to make crossover rap. This resulted in a backlash wherein rappers began to cry foul at the pop-rap trend, and the revolution which came would come to a head during the Summer of 1990.

In the Summer of 1990, Bell Biv Devoe's "Poison," MC Hammer's "U Can't Touch This," and Snap!'s "The Power," all reached the top of multiple charts. That same summer saw the release of Vanilla Ice's "Ice Ice Baby," Candyman's "Knockin' Boots," and Dee-Lite's dance hit "Groove Is In The Heart." At the same time, Technotronic's "This Beat Is Technotronic" climbed the club charts, and Madonna's "Vogue," which had hit #1 at the tail end of spring, further popularized the international club/house music domination of the Pop and R&B Charts. Collectively, these events lead to some infighting inside the world of black music as a whole.

I've written about the beef between hip Hop/rap heads, R&B/ New Jack Swing fans, & and house/club music kids (which first reared its ugly head in early 1990) in an essay called "Born Into The 90's © R.Kelly & The Public Announcement" (originally published on my old blog Bastard Swordsman piece). Between the Summer of 1988, when New Jack Swing took over R&B, and 1989, when house and freestyle acts gained larger mainstream followings, there was still harmony amongst all of these different black music fans when they were in a club setting. However, once international club music took over the charts and rap began to crossover — while New Jack Swing was looming larger and larger — the fans began to butt heads in public.

1990 also marked a the time when house music experienced its own sea changes. Within the pantheon of black music, house music had become progressively more popular with each passing year since 1986. And Since beginning in 1988, it was outwardly acknowledged and incorporated into rap music via Chicago's "hip house" movement, usurping Go Go, which was the music form of choice in the DMV area (Washington D.C., Maryland and Virginia). By 1990, house music was going in a different direction after house/club music went mainstream. Pal Joey produced two house music classics that changed everything that year: Earth People's "Dance" and Soho's "Hot Music." "Dance" was a precursor to the soulful, uptempo house music that took off in France and influenced Daft Punk, Dmitri From Paris, Cassius & Justice; and "Hot Music" captured the attention of house and hip hop production fans entranced with the sampling "edits" or "chops" utilized in creating it. Those obsessed with "Hot Music" had to purchase SP 1200's and other drum machines; they were on a mission to discover how to make beats just like it. Rappers freestyled over it for years and it even changed the way house heads and "circle kids" danced. They were each revolutionary productions for different reasons that planted seeds of influence worldwide.

Hip hop heads began to get increasingly vocal about how house music and New Jack Swing seemed to be diluting the sound of rap in 1990. They expressed their anger over the new trend of "pop rap" that catered to a crossover audience, and they were especially sick of the looming influence of club music-rap hybrids. Whereas "hip house" was acceptable in years previous (i.e. Jungle Brothers "I'll House You" or KYZE "Stomp (Move Jump Jack Your Body)"), groups like Snap! (who had Turbo B) and Technotronic (whose rappers were Ya Kid K and MC Eric) were frowned upon. Autumn, 1990 only brought more of the same for these distraught rap fans.

In September 1990, two UK producers used Soul II Soul as their blueprint and crafted a club/dance friendly version of Suzanne Vega's "Tom's Diner," and the song began to creep up the charts. Then, in October 1990 C + C Music Factory released their debut single, "Gonna Make You Sweat (Everybody Dance Now)." Not only did it take off immediately, thanks largely to Martha Wash's vocals (she also did the vocals for Black Box, but she was uncredited for both) but they featured a rapper by the name of Freedom Williams.

Rap fans were distraught, especially after Vanilla Ice's "Ice Ice Baby" managed to knock Janet Jackson's "Black Cat" off the top of the Billboard charts (November 3rd, 1990). In 1989, Tone Loc's "Wild Thing" had peaked at #2 and "Funky Cold Medina" peaked at #3, while Young MC's "Bust A Move" stalled at #7. MC Hammer's "U Can't Touch This" peaked at #8, due to it initially only being available to purchase as a 12" single. But in the end, it would be Vanilla Ice who would laid lay claim to the elusive top Billboard spot. Afterwards, the proverbial shit hit the metaphorical fan. And the FANS...

The backlash against MC Hammer and Vanilla Ice intensified with each of their successes. Every time a rap song became popular and crossed over, rap fans became more and more torn. They wanted rap to be bigger, but as its white fan base grew (exponentially through several factors I identified in my essay "How Touré Failed Hip-Hop & America"), they also worried about rap becoming soft and compromising itself in order to crossover. While rap fans were tentative with rap's newfound popularity, there were numerous classic rap albums released that same year which that compromised nothing sonically new, nor in terms of lyrical content.

All throughout 1990 notable and classic rap albums were released, including: Eric B. & Rakim's Let The Rhythm Hit 'Em, Public Enemy's Fear Of A Black Planet, EPMD's Business As Usual, Kool G. Rap & DJ Polo's Wanted: Dead Or Alive, Ice Cube's Amerikkka's Most Wanted, Boogie Down Productions' Edutainment, Brand Nubian's One For All, Poor Righteous Teachers' Holy Intellect, X-Clan's To The East, Blackwards, A Tribe Called Quest's People's Instinctive Travels & The Paths Of Rhythm, Salt N' Pepa's Black's Magic, Kid N' Play's Funhouse, Monie Love's Down To Earth, LL Cool J's Mama Said Knock You Out, Too Short's Short Dog's In The House, Digital Underground's Sex Packets, Compton Most Wanted's It's A Compton Thang, Above The Law's Livin' Like Hustlers, and King Tee's At Your Own Risk. Collectively, these albums alone speak to the diversity and balance in mainstream rap at the time the rap music scene was going through turmoil.

Albums like Lord Finesse & DJ Mike Smooth's Funky Technician laid down the groundwork for Nas to release Illmatic four years later. Tragedy, the man who was Nas before Nas, released his debut album as Intelligent Hoodlum. Kwamé dropped his sophomore album A Day In The Life: A Pokedelik Adventure. Masta Ace and D-Nice both released their debut albums. Lakim Shabazz released The Lost Tribe Of Shabazz, his sophomore offering produced by DJ Mark The 45 King. And as DJ Mark The

45 King blessed our ears with his album 45 Kingdom. While all of this great music was being released, it was being overshadowed by the fact that MC Hammer and Vanilla Ice was raking in money from sales and endorsement deals, thanks to their pop friendly rap, and the fact that Club music was invading the rap world.

At the end of 1990, C+C Music Factory released their LP Gonna Make You Sweat, which shot up the charts. Technotronic, Snap!, and Black Box dominated the radio and video channels all year long, racking up crazy record sales along the way. Bell Biv Devoe's "Hip hop smoothed out on the R&B tip with a Pop feel appeal to it" resulted in double Platinum sales of Poison, with 3 Billboard hits on multiple charts by the time the year ended. MC Hammer's Please Hammer Don't Hurt 'Em and Vanilla Ice's To The Extreme sold in excess of 10 million copies combined; and Vanilla Ice's album was the fastest selling rap album of all times up until then, which really pissed people off — in large part because it was a mediocre project overall.

1990 closed with Monie Love's infectious Monie In The Middle" being knocked off the top of the rap charts by New Jack Swing rapper Father M.C.'s Ill Do 4 U, which featured a young Mary J. Blige on background vocals. It was Father M.C.'s 2nd #1 Rap hit, the first being "Treat Them Like They Want To Be Treated," which was produced by Prince Markie Dee and Mark Rooney under the direction of Uptown/MCA's Andre Harrell and his young protegé Sean "Puff Daddy" Combs. Meanwhile, LL Cool J's R&B-tinged single "Around The Way Girl," produced by Marley Marl, was steadily climbing up the Rap, Dance, and billboard Hot 100 charts since it's release in late November.

Facing the temptation of widespread appeal, more money, and of outside influences in 1990, the rap world had to find a way to deal with their newfound commercial viability while maintaining the integrity of the music and the culture Kid N' Play hit it big with a movie called House Party that year, while Will "The Fresh

Prince" Smith and "Jazzy" Jeff Townes now had their own Quincy Jones produced hit TV series on NBC called "The Fresh Prince Of Bel Air." That same year, LL Cool J had landed his first official acting role as a cop in the film "The Hard Way" (which officially came out in early 1991). This what ultimately outdone by Ice T's role as a cop in the movie New Jack City. Although Ice T shot his role in New York in the Spring/Summer of 1990, the movie wasn't released until early 1991. Times were indeed a-changin'...

Soon, MC Hammer and Vanilla Ice would both have action figures bearing their likenesses. And while MC Hammer began filming for his own VHS tape, Vanilla Ice was set to appear in both the sequel to Teenage Mutant Ninja Turtles and his own film vehicle to be released the next year. MC Hammer was endorsing every product possible while other popular rappers had trouble locking down one. At the same time, the emergence of the Freedom Williams fronted C+C Music Factory meant that labels would potentially be looking to push emcees to rap over music that would endear them to the Club MTV audience.

Due to a perfect storm of television shows that included "Yo! MTV Raps," "The Arsenio Hall Show," "In Living Color," and "The Fresh Prince Of Bel Air" plus the success of the movie House Party, MC Hammer, and Vanilla Ice, the entire terrain around rap music changed. Rap was finally being embraced by the mainstream and it was reflected in its newfound widespread marketability. Rap's music's fan base was becoming increasingly larger and whiter. Hip hop dance classes were now regularly offered in the suburbs due to these factors. And the controversy surrounding hardcore/Gangsta Rap and sexually charged rap music with explicit lyrics, like the kind popularized by 2 Live Crew, had also drawn in young white kids who saw it as a form of rebellion.

Afrocentric/Conscious Rap, such as Paris's The Devil Made Me Do It album, was thriving next to Hardcore/Gangsta Rap. The Nation Of Gods & Earths were still highly influential and the Native Tongues collective (A Tribe Called Quest, De La Soul, Queen Latifah, Black Sheep, Monie Love, and Jungle Brothers) expanded their hold on the rap world after A Tribe Called Quest and Monie Love had released their debut albums. Special Ed, Run-DMC, Big Daddy Kane, D-Nice, Grandaddy I.U., King Sun & K-Solo all dropped notable projects as well. There was plenty of balance in the rap world, but only now the lure of crossover appeal loomed overhead large where the opportunity was once limited. It was wide open now.

In previous years, it was easy to determine if a rapper was selling out, but things were blurred in 1990. For example, The Fat Boys made songs like "Wipe Out" and "The Twist" in order to cross over. Run-DMC to make made "Walk This Way" with Aerosmith, giving Run-DMC a wider audience. At this time in rap, Ice Cube could go platinum in two months without a radio single off and just one video. The only charting single off Amerikkka's Most Wanted hit #1 on the Rap charts but never appeared on the Billboard Hot 100.

And it's worth noting that at this time, Ice Cube had just as many, if not more, white fans buying his music as crossover rappers had. Meanwhile, Kwamé and Kid N' Play were making hits being themselves. But were they selling out because their music was more commercially viable and radio friendly? They still couldn't outsell Ice Cube, and a Hardcore/Gangsta Rap group like Above The Law actually had MORE #1 Billboard Rap hits in 1990 than Salt N' Pepa, Kid N' Play, or and Kwame did. Lines were blurring and the game had changed.

Both rappers and fans alike harbored trepidation approaching what was previously uncharted territory. It took just over a decade for the genre to finally be acknowledged by mainstream award shows like the Grammys and the American Music Awards. Everyone was leery of selling out or, better yet, being perceived of attempting to try to sell out. If you used R&B, New Jack Swing, house or club music as a means to make your music more commercially viable, you faced the possibility of being scrutinized by your peers. If you made straight up rap but crossed over anyways, you could still experience backlash due to jealousy. It all boiled down to respect…

Another interesting fact worth noting is that beginning in October 1990, a brand new hip hop radio show first aired in New York on WKCR 89.9 @ Columbia University. The show, which featured a white DJ named Skinny Bones (later known as Stretch Armstrong), a Puerto Rican dude named Bobbito Garcia, and their boy, an Puerto Rican/Cubn kid from Uptown known as Kurious Jorge. This show would evolve over time to become The Stretch Armstrong & Bobbito Show and become extremely influential in the rap music world. 1990 was a transition year in every way you can imagine…

1991:
Rap's Other Forgotten Transition Year

After we all successfully weathered the tumultuous year that was 1990, several events took place in the world of music in 1991 that ultimately led to the perfect storm which birthed rap's 2nd Golden Era at the top of 1992.

As we enter 1991, we're still deeply entrenched in what we considered the Pop Rap Era. There was this hysteria amongst rap fans that the genre would become watered down and overly commercialized. Whereas in years past house music and R&B seemed to perfectly complement Rap and they coexisted in relative harmony, tensions came to a head during this time period.

A byproduct of this strife spilled into the club scene where the hip hop heads, R&B/New Jack Swing contingency, and the house/club crowd converged. The most awkward part was some who were part of each group had to choose a side, since the rap kids slowly became undesirables in the club scene. (If you're seeking any further information on this internal strife within the world of Black music, I previously covered it in my essays A B-Boy's Alpha and Born Into The '90s. Both essays are included in this collection.) As we entered 199, the hottest rap songs out, chart wise, were Gerardo's "Rico Suave" and Father MC's "I'll Do 4 U." One was dance-floor oriented rap with a New Jack Swingesque aesthetic, while the other was clearly crossover danceable rap lite. Gerardo was never embraced by the rap world, he was seen more as a novelty act, so he didn't receive the same bile that had already been directed towards MC Hammer and Vanilla Ice. That anger was instead reserved for any rap act that seemed like they were trying to water down their sound and chase crossover success.

There are several reasons 1991 stands alone as a crucial year for the future of not only rap but music in general. This is the year that the burgeoning power and overall influence of black music was made apparent to everyone. While the increasing drawing power of black film and the widespread appeal of black music was being made apparent, as black themed television shows were bringing in huge ratings, many still didn't believe — and tried to downplay or outright ignore — the commercial viability or influence of Black music and art on the industry at large. As we entered the Soundscan Era on March 1st, 1991, that became harder to do. As Soundscan guidelines were implemented in regards to the Hot 100 and Billboard 200, it the popularity of Dance, Club, R&B, and Rap music became clear.

In 1990, the Kid N' Play movie vehicle House Party established the drawing power of black films, but what it failed to do was sell units of the original soundtrack. By 1991, there was a new wave of black films that were created by the commercial success of House Party and several profitable Black studio films and video rentals. This resulted in a mini Black film renaissance beginning in 1991. It was kicked off with the release of the film New Jack City and its corresponding soundtrack.

The New Jack City OST was released on March 5th, 1991 and proved to be a game changer as it ended up becoming the top selling album on the Billboard R&B album charts for 8 straight weeks (April 27, 1991 to June 15, 1991). At one point, the New Jack City OST even shot up as high as the 2nd spot on Billboard's Top 200 Albums chart, as the film did surprisingly well at the box office. When it was all said and done, the soundtrack boasted four hit singles: (Color Me Badd's "I Wanna Sex You Up," Christopher Williams's "I'm Dreamin'," Troop and LeVert f/Queen Latifah "For The Love Of Money/Living For The City," and Ice T's "New Jack Hustler."

It would soon be followed by such film soundtracks as Boyz N The Hood, The Five Heartbeats, Jungle Fever, House Party 2, Uptown/MCA's Strictly Business, and Def Jam's Livin' Large!. Of these soundtracks, Jungle Fever would spend two consecutive weeks atop the R&B Albums chart, while the Boyz N The Hood OST would spend the entire month of September as the top selling R&B album, powered by three hit singles: Compton's Most Wanted's "Growin' Up In The Hood" (which was the #1 Billboard Rap single the week of September 7th, 1991), Tevin Campbell f/Chubb Rock's "Just Ask Me To," and Tony! Toni! Toné!'s "Me & You."

Another key development of 1991 was N.W.A.'s "Efil4zaggin" making it to the #1 selling album on the Billboard Hot 200 album chart on June 22, 1991. This opened up the eyes of the industry, considering that N.W.A. had none of the obvious crossover appeal of MC Hammer or Vanilla Ice. In 1990, MC Hammer's Please Hammer, Don't Hurt 'Em held the #1 spot on the Billboard Hot 200 album charts for 21 total weeks (18 straight). And it was Vanilla Ice knocked him off the top spot was for the final 8 weeks of 1990. It shouldn't have been much of a surprise to the music industry, considering the fact that rap albums were the top selling ones for 29 weeks of the 52 weeks of 1990 and the first 8 weeks of 1991.

More proof of the emerging dominance of black music and non-rock music genres over rock was evident, as either R&B/soul/pop or club/house songs held the top spot on the Hot 100 for 28 of the remaining 44 weeks of 1991, post the inception of the Soundscan Era in March. The first #1 rap song on the Hot 100 Billboard Charts of this era was Marky Mark & The Funky Bunch's Good Vibrations; it took the #1 spot for the week of October 5th, 1991. Some thought it was an anomaly, that is until P.M. Dawn's Set Adrift Of Memory Bliss also reached the top position for the week of November 30th, 1991.

In Derek Thompson's piece in The Atlantic titled "In 1991, Rap Changed Pop Music Forever" (May 8th, 2015), he cited several cursory reasons why rap music forever changed pop music while completely failing to go in depth about exactly why and what the byproducts were, or even acknowledging the influence of black music had on the larger music industry at the time. The piece instead took a left turn into a discussion of statistics and chord progressions. There was no mention of the fact that black culture had recently captured the cultural zeitgeist, ca. 1991. Incidentally, this was also apparent in the sudden rise of reggae and its return to the black music and mainstream charts.

Beginning in 1990 and continuing into 1991, Reggae artists like Maxi Priest ("Close To You"), Beres Hammond ("Tempted To Touch"), Mad Cobra, Wayne Wonder, Ninjaman, Tony Rebel, Daddy Freddy, Papa San, Super Cat, Tiger, Cutty Ranks ("The Stopper"), and others began to gain more of a foothold on the UK music charts than they did stateside. These popular Reggae artists were played more and more in parties which resulted in dancehall reggae songs getting regular placement on mixtapes. Then reggae sets became a regular occurrence in clubs, where the dances began to spread. Reggae's growing influence in the context of black American music resulted in it becoming featured more and more on rap recordings in 1991, and for one of its main superstars, Shabba Ranks, to get signed to a major label.

Shabba Ranks's major label debut, As Raw As Ever, was released on May 21, 1991 to overwhelming critical acclaim and fan reaction. The album also became a commercial success by topping the Billboard R&B Albums chart on the week of November 9, 1991, behind his hit singles "Trailer Load A Girls" and "House Call," which featured Maxi Priest. On January 30, 1992 it As Raw As Ever received a Gold certification plaque from the RIAA, signaling that it had sold in excess of 500,000 units. Shabba Ranks's success resulted in reggae officially taking its place within the black American music market, and it paved the way for reggae artists like Super Cat, Daddy Freddy, Patra, Mad Cobra, Tiger, Jamal-Ski, and others getting major label deals heading into 1992.

N.W.A's top selling album Efil4zaggin featured reggae artist Admiral Dancehall on two tracks ("Alwayz Into Somethin'" and "Dayz Of Wayback"). Shabba Ranks had a single with KRS One called "The Jam" (which eventually became a #1 single on the Rap charts); and Heavy D & The Boyz did the song "Body & Mind" featuring Daddy Freddy. By the time 1991 was over, reggae and rap would begin to merge into the hybrid genre of hip hop reggae, where reggae artists would chat or toast over rap production. Hip hop reggae would usurp New Jack Swing/R&B rap and ultimately oust house/club music-flavored rap out altogether going into 1992 and beyond.

International club music and house continued to thrive throughout 1991, as acts like Black Box, Dee-Lite, C & C Music Factory, Enigma, Stereo MC's, EMF, The KLF, Londonbeat, Jomanda, Crystal Waters, CeCe Peniston, Cathy Dennis and Adeva all had huge hits on both radio and in the club. Their success filtered into realms of R&B, as Lisa Lisa & Cult Jam tapped C & C Music Factory for the production of their huge hit "Let The Beat Hit 'Em."

Not only did "Let The Beat Hit 'Em" spend three consecutive weeks atop the Dance charts (July 13th to July 27, 1991) and a week at #1 on the R&B charts (September 14, 1991), but it reached all the way up to #37 on the Billboard Hot 100. It would be the last hit Lisa Lisa & Cult Jam would ever have. (The group disbanded shortly afterwards.) As 1991 moved towards the end of the year, the international club/house music sound began to get really tiring and repetitive, especially as Reggae gained more ground within the realm of Black music.

In April 1991, Massive Attack would release their debut LP "Blue Lines," following their singles "Daydreaming" and

"Unfinished Sympathy". This new exciting genre of music coming out of the UK would gain more and more attention from music fans stateside, via UK music magazines, college radio, and late night video shows. This music would later be called "Trip Hop". Simultaneously, a new sound, later called grunge or alternative rock, began to gain steam in rock circles, behind a band called Nirvana, who had released their debut album Nevermind in September 1991. It would gain exponentially more and more steam throughout 1992, further cutting into international club and House music's overall appeal.

The death knell of the dissipating influence and waning popularity of international club and house sounding music became more evident when MTV canceled their long running show "Club MTV" in June 1992 and replaced it with "The Grind," a show with a playlist of R&B, rap, reggae, and the occasional club fare. At this point, where the mainstays of the popular hybrid sounds? Technotronic? Dead. Black Box? Dead. Snap!? DEAD! C & C Music Factory? Barely hanging on…

1991 was also crucial in regards to rap for a number of other reasons, all of which lead directly to another Golden Era. First, the early beginnings of the East Coast/West Coast feud can possibly be traced back to the fallout from an episode of "Yo! MTV Raps," where Fab 5 Freddy asked DJ Quik and 2nd II None to freestyle and they all declined stating they didn't do it. Since DJ Quik's album on dropped January 15th, 1991 I can guess his appearance on "Yo! MTV Raps" had to happen that month, which would've prompted Tim Dog to diss him on his song "Fuck Compton," which was released shortly thereafter in March 1991.

While N.W.A and DJ Quik both received RIAA plaques and Compton's Most Wanted racked up numerous hits and widespread acclaim throughout 1991, Tim Dog's diss scored him a #1 Billboard Rap hit for the week of October 12, 1991. His album *Penicillin On Wax* dropped the next month and is considered one of the most underrated rap albums of the '90's. Second, the advent of the VHS promo tape. Since Rap artists were becoming more and more commercially viable — some even getting roles in films — it only made sense that record labels would instead opt to give them promotional VHS' (video tapes) rather than foot the bill for a full length studio film.

Kool Moe Dee's "Funke Funke Wisdom" VHS promo tape dropped the week before his album did in June 1991. MC Hammer's label Capitol Records dropped his short film Please Hammer Don't Hurt Em: The Movie in July 1991. Ice T released a short film version of his album O.G. Original Gangster in August 1991; it featured videos for each song on the album. Jive/Zomba also released the VHS promo tape "Boogie Down Productions: Live" before releasing the live BDP album Live Hardcore Worldwide in 1991. Certainly, VHS promo tapes made a lot more sense than sinking millions of dollars into a full length film with a soundtrack that can both flop, like what happened to SBK's Vanilla Ice film vehicle Cool As Ice.

Third, the debuts of pivotal rap artists. One of the key reasons that 1991 paved the way for 1992 kicking off another Golden Era lies in the fact that numerous classic albums were released during this year and it also featured either the outright debut of several key players in the world of rap and/or their debut projects. A short list of artists and groups who either released their debut albums in 1991 or made their first appearances includes Main Source (Large Professor); Nas (on "Live From The BBQ" off the Main Source album Breaking Atoms); Cormega (as MC Cor on "Set It Off" from PHD (Poet x Hot Day) "Without Warning"); GZA/Genius (Words From The Genius), RZA (as Prince Rakeem); DJ Quik; Leaders Of The New School; Black Sheep; KMD (DOOM); Del The Funkee Homosapien; The Fu Schnickens (Ring The Alarm); Pete Rock & C.L. Smooth (All Souled Out EP); The UMC's Freestyle Fellowship (To Whom It May Concern); Showbiz &

A.G. (Soul Clap EP); Naughty By Nature; Cypress Hill; Edo.G & Da Bulldogs; Kid Capri ("The Tape"); Organized Konfusion; O.C (on "Fudge Pudge" off the Organized Konfusion album Organized Konfusion; DMX (as DMX The Great winning "Unsigned Hype" in The Source magazine); MC Breed & The DFC; 2 Pac (on "Same Song" off Digital Underground's This Is An EP Release & and 2Pacalypse Now); 8 Ball & MJG (Listen To The Lyrics); Coolio (as part of W.C. & The MAAD Circle); Master P (Get Away Clean) and The Coup (The EP).

Fourth, the emergence of alternative rap. The popularity of hardcore rap and the commercial viability of danceable, pop-tinged radio friendly rap converged with the last vestiges of militant/Afrocentric/Conscious/NGE-themed rap in 1991. Record labels sought to try to introduce alternative rap to the fold in hopes of cashing in on the burgeoning genre. They'd seek out acts that would appeal to those who might be put off by "angry" rap. Music fans seeking something more "positive" and uplifting that wasn't dance centered but still possessed the same intensity, social commentary, and consciousness of Public Enemy sans the rage. Also they hoped to possibly rope in the college radio crowd as well as those who were into experimental forms of music but not necessarily Rap fans.

Canadian rap group Dream Warriors' 1990 singles on 4th & Broadway/Island "Wash Your Face In My Sink" and "My Definition Of A Boombastic Jazz Style" both gained steam in early 1991 and paved the way for Gee Street/Island group P.M. Dawn's Set Adrift On Memory Bliss to have a lane. Gee Street's Stereo MC's single "Elevate My Mind" also gained traction stateside which made other major labels also take a serious look at signing "alternative" rap acts. Epic Records signed HanSoul ("Imagination") and Chrysalis/EMI signed a group called Arrested Development, who scored a huge hit with their song "Tennessee" and their six-times platinum debut album 3 Years, 5 Months and

2 Days in the Life Of... Qwest/Warner Bros. released QD III's Soundlab album, which featured a Q-Tip soundalike named Justin Warfield ("Season Of The Vic"), who would go on to be a pioneer in the genre. 4th Broadway/Island signed the Michael Franti fronted Disposable Heroes Of Hiphoprisy which led to Joe "The Butcher" Nicolo signing Philadelphia's conscious/alternative rap group The Goats then releasing their album the next year. RCA Records signee Me Phi Me also released his album in early 1992. Unfortunately, for most of these groups, the sea changes that took place at the beginning of 1992 pretty much either buried most of them as soon as their projects dropped or ensured that their success would be short lived or wouldn't last as the second Golden Era of rap progressed.

Another factor that fueled the interest in alternative rap was the overwhelmingly positive response to MTV's "Yo! MTV Raps Unplugged" show, which aired on May 1, 1991. A band called Pop's Cool Love backed up A Tribe Called Quest, MC Lyte, LL Cool J, and De La Soul in front of a live audience. Watching the combination of emcees with a live band launched an explosion of "Hip Hop bands" that would later be given even more credence by the ruling in the Grand Upright copyright infringement lawsuit against Biz Markie that would be handed down at the end of the year. (For more information of this pivotal sampling and copyright infringement lawsuit, see Amir Said's book The Art of Sampling.)

1991 was a year chock full of essential, seminal and classic rap albums. Among them being A Tribe Called Quest The Low End Theory, Main Source Breaking Atoms, Ice T O.G. Original Gangster, Ice Cube Death Certificate, KMD Mr. Hood, Scarface Mr. Scarface Is Back, DJ Quik Quik Is The Name, Leaders Of The New School A Future Without A Past, Nice & Smooth Aint A Damn Thing Changed, Edo.G & Da Bulldogs Life Of A Kid In The Ghetto, Del The Funkee Homosapien I Wish My Brother George Was Here, Digital Underground Sons Of The P, Public

Enemy Apocalypse 91: The Enemy Strikes Black, Geto Boys We Can't Be Stopped, 3rd Bass Derelicts Of Dialect, Chubb Rock The One, Slick Rick The Ruler's Back, Organized Konfusion S/T Organize Konfusion, N.W.A Efil4zaggin, De La Soul De La Soul Is Dead, Black Sheep A Wolf In Sheep's Clothing, Compton's Most Wanted Straight Check N' Em, and Cypress Hill S/T Cypress Hill among others.

One album released from 1991 had so much significance that it forever changed the course of rap music. On August 27, 1991 Biz Markie's third album I Need A Haircut was released. It contained a song that never received proper sample clearance or licensing to be included on the project. This resulted in a lawsuit that forever changed rap music and subsequent clearance guidelines for rap albums. [For a detailed examination of sampling and copyright infringement lawsuit, see Amir Said's book The Art of Sampling.]

As 1991 came to a close, Ice Cube's Death Certificate was the top selling album on the R&B charts for the final three weeks of the year (December 14 through the 28) by fending off both Prince & The New Power Generation's Diamonds & Pearls and Jodeci's Forever My Lady. The UMC's "Blue Cheese" spent the final two weeks of 1991 atop the Hot Rap Singles chart, while U2's Achtung Baby and Michael Jackson's Dangerous were the top selling Pop albums. Few things are more telling than the fact that, as we close out 1991, both Michael Jackson and Prince had finally embraced incorporating rap in their music. Michael Jackson had features from Heavy D on "Jam," A+ (of Wreckx N Effect) on "She Drives Me Wild," and some terrible verse from producer Bill Bottrell as L.T.B. on "Black Or White." Prince actually opted to rhyme himself on "Gett Off," while previously producing for rappers Monie Love, Robin Power, Carmen Electra, TC Ellis; and having Tony G kick verses on his album. That two of Pop's biggest names were finally recognizing the inevitable rise of hip hop/rap had to be a foreshadow of what was to come.

How The Buzz Around Niki Minaj's Debut Demonstrates the Rap Game On Steroids

When Nicki Minaj's Pink Friday made the rounds with the bloggerati its first week back in 2002, the general consensus is was that Nicki Minaj's Pink Friday sucked. But the project's buzz was enormous. Nicki Minaj had broken a Billboard record for having the most songs on the Billboard Hot 100 at the same time. In any other era of music history, this accomplishment would actually be impressive, but in this era it's not so impressive.

Nicki Minaj received co-signs from everyone with a name in the music industry, as well as accolades from everyone you could possibly imagine, all before her debut album even dropped. And she had a documentary set to air on MTV around the same time of the release. Now that the culmination of all that hard work and overwhelming industry hype is a piece of flaming hot garbage, it's time to retrace our steps and figure out how the supposed savior of female emcees got to her place as a media darling in the first place.

I'd been hearing Nicki Minaj via her mixtape appearances since 2006 via AllHipHop.com and Boxden, but I never once took her serious because, regardless of the pictures that I saw of her online, as I was never impressed with her bars or her music. Eventually, Nicki got with Lil' Wayne and his Young Money imprint. In August, 2009, it was made official and Nicki Minaj signed a deal with Young Money/Universal. As soon as that signing became official, "the push" went into overdrive. With a corporate machine behind her, the co-sign of "the greatest rapper alive" Lil' Wayne, in addition to the recent Young Money acquisition of Drake, her signing became more of an event. You also have to take into account that Nicki Minaj was pretty much the lone female emcee in the industry. Due to her business and industry relationships and crew affiliation, she was automatically tied to damn near everyone in the industry with a heartbeat.

Niki Minaj was also in that rare space of being one of the few artists in the industry that was legitimately considered "hot", so when people in the industry went looking for featured guests where did they go first? To put all of Nicki Minaj's features and guest appearances into perspective, when Jay-Z was in the studio with Robin Thicke doing "Meiple,", Robin Thicke mentioned that he had a record that needed something extra and Jay-Z himself suggested Nicki Minaj to him for the song that became "Shake It For Daddy." Jay fuckin' Z. The God MC. Former president of Def Jam Records. Let that marinate.

Being that the entire industry was (is) in dire straits and everyone is was looking for a hit, they were going to reach out for whoever was the hottest at the moment for features. It happened with T-Pain and Akon when they were on everyone's hooks, and it often resulted in them being on 5 five or more songs at a time in rotation on the radio. Also consider the fact that Nicki Minaj was the only female emcee that was even relevant at the major label level, which would inevitably get her even more work.

We also have to factor in the fact that the radio only plays 20 damn songs in its rotation at any given time. This is how Nicki Minaj was able to have so many songs on the Billboard Hot 100 simultaneously. In essence, it's akin to when in the '90s all of a sudden multiple Major League baseball players began having 40+ home run seasons simultaneously, when before it was considered impressive when a player hit more than 25 in a season. Later on, it was discovered that these players were taking performance enhancing drugs, so this whole stretch of broken records was achieved through artificial means.

Since Nicki was hot and the only game in town in an industry with only five to eight artists moving units, it's safe to say that the entire rap game was on steroids (metaphorically speaking) at the time Nicki Minaj's debut studio album. Nicki Minaj's buzz was tied into so many surrounding factors regarding her being all over the radio, all over the print media and the rap blogosphere, that when the industry co-signs came in there was an inevitable backlash from some hip hop heads. Those of us who had listened to female rappers with superior talent (rappers who got no shine) saw this push develop and knew that the backlash would come.

Nicki Minaj raised her profile by taking racy pictures, playing up her possible bisexuality, calling herself a Barbie, rapping in ridiculous accents, and changing her delivery as if she was schizophrenic during songs. She also developed this off-the-wall image that includes ridiculous wigs and over the top costumes. It's as if being herself and relying strictly on the quality of her bars in the industry wasn't (isn't) enough. Who are we kidding? It isn't, otherwise Lady Gaga would just perform under her government name.

In any event, Nicki Minaj built up a devoted cult following of "Barbies" that dress up like her and recite her bars. Nicki Minaj was (and still is) 75% image. And let's discuss her actual talent for once, shall we? On the mic, Nicki Minaj is mediocre at best. She does have some occasional flashes of brilliance and from time to time she will spit a clever line, but these occurrences are few and far between. I don't care how good you look or how fat your ass is when I'm listening to your music. I judge strictly on talent. That being the case, Nicki Minaj falls short with me.

Talent wise, Nicki Minaj doesn't warrant the level of attention or praise she received from critics, industry heads, and artists alike. When you have Kanye West saying dangerous things like Nicki Minaj could be one of the greatest artists ever, or when people compare Nicki Minaj to Lauryn Hill (in her prime), you need to step back and do knowledge to exactly what's taking place. MTV aired a documentary about Nicki Minaj called "My Time Is Now" on November 28, 2010. The last time MTV did a documentary for an album release was for her label mate Drake. Coincidence?

Didn't Steve Rifkind also say on record that Asher Roth's Asleep In The Bread Aisle would be a hip hop classic and a game changer a year before Nicki Minaj's debut album? Who even remembers that damn album now? When's the last time anyone even played it? In the first decade of the 200s, The rap game was in its steroids era and the media was BALCO. The media hype machine in tandem with corporate entities pushed out these mediocre artists to the masses. And they still do this, and time and again it blows up in their faces when the final product is mediocre. Mediocre talent produces mediocre music. It's mathematics, God.

The tired practice of pursuing "hotness" or artificially generating it is tiresome. It's also transparent when certain entertainers or entities attempt to keep themselves "hot" or maintain their "relevance" by attaching themselves to whomever is hot at the time. Here, I'm specifically speaking of Diddy. Jay Electronica went and signed with Roc Nation instead of with Bad Boy. If Diddy stopped being a Bugatti Boy with Rick Ross and dancing in Nicki's videos maybe things would've gone differently. By the way, Diddy also co-signed Nicki Minaj. He also said that Rick Ross is the new Biggie Smalls so his credibility is shot.

So here we were in November, 2010. Nicki Minaj was all over the radio. She was all over the newsstand. She was all over the television. Her name was on the lips of everyone with a name worth mentioning. Her album was highly anticipated and expectations were sky high. But the album hits music journalists, critics, bloggers, fans and it was met with less than favorable reactions. The general consensus was that the album is was schizophrenic and sounded like a mediocre collection of radio singles and club, songs as opposed to a concise album. But was Is this really a surprise to anyone?

We are still in an era where image is valued far more than actual talent and creativity. We are still in an era where mediocrity is rewarded and excellence is frowned upon for fear that it won't be understood or that it may be too hard to market. We are still in an era where record labels, music publications, and mass media are desperate for superstars. So much so that they're willing to manufacture them through whatever means they have available to them.

In 2010 and the first couple of years thereafter, Nicki Minaj was killing the game. A game where she had absolutely no competition. A game where everyone was helping her out by feeding her the ball every possession; and when she did score they all remarked that she's one of the greatest ever to do it. A game where her jersey is the only one being sold at the arena. A game where the referees have been told to not call her for double dribbling, traveling, or offensive fouls. A game she's essentially been guaranteed to win.

The Quintessential Definition
of A Backpacker

If you've ever been on a music related message board before or on in a hip hop thread on Twitter or some other social media network, you've seen the word "backpacker". If you've ever heard the word/term used as a description or a derogatory term (i.e. Fuck you fake-ass bitch, Lupe Fiasco lovin' niggas! Y'all need to take that backpack bullshit back to the suburbs and listen to some real shit like Young Jeezy!) and wondered what the hell it meant or even where it came from, I'll explain it to you in this essay. This essay is not just about where the term came from, it's also about the grand Kansas City Shuffle executed by the government approving the Telecommunications Act and Viacom, Emmis Communications, and Clear Channel in the roles of The Boss, The Rabbi, Mr. Goodkat, and Slevin Kelevra. (If you haven't yet seen the movie Lucky Number Slevin, do so...it will all make perfect sense then).

Let us begin....at the beginning. There was a time when if you didn't at least make an effort to speak about issues or put a conscious cut on your album, you were clowned incessantly. (Ask LL Cool J or any kid that rocked in African medallion back in the day for the same reason.). At one point, being Afrocentric or conscious was mainstream. That changed over time and we entered the '90s. 1990 was a transition year and hip hop was searching for a new direction. 1991 brought that direction, style, and a bunch of new talent to the forefront (along with mad classic albums). Everything fell into place the following year, though.

After 1991 had brought the hip hop world a new influx of hip hop groups, style changes, and classic albums, 1992 turned into

54

what was called The Year Of The Underground by most hip hop publications (especially The Source). That year Das Efx, Redman, EPMD, Dr. Dre, Snoop Dogg, Pete Rock & C.L. Smooth, Black Sheep, The UMCs, Fu-Schnickens, Cypress Hill, House Of Pain, Del The Funkee Homosapien, Mobb Deep, UGK, Common, 2Pac, Diamond, The Pharcyde, etc. all dropped debut projects, and either did big numbers, made a classic LP/single, and/or dominated the charts. Plus, they were all different.

Some were super lyrical, some just spit party rhymes. They were diverse in their styles and influences, some wore crazy ass clothes, others rocked work gear, hoodies, BDUs, and Timberlands boots most of the time. Some rhymed about space-age shit and others came up with straight up street tales, and others spit battle rhymes. It didn't matter what approach they took to the music or where they were from, they were all regarded as hip hoppers/rappers. And oh yeah, a lot of them often rocked backpacks.

Whether it was Grand Puba (who popularized the look when he wore a backpack in his lead single and video for his 1st solo LP "Reel To Reel"), Leaders Of The New School, Das Efx, Black Sheep, Redman, Black Moon, Ruff House Survivors (who had a single called "Check Da Backpack"), Mobb Deep or Onyx, heads — from the corniest to the grimiest — used to rock backpacks. You could keep all your shit in them! Your rhyme book, your black book (for graf), your contact information, your weed, guns, knives, pens, money, whatever! Rockin' a backpack wasn't an issue at all. Hip Hop also began invading the mainstream, moving units and becoming more and more popular with the youth across the board. This was mostly because of industry fallout, which was due to the crossover appeal of Dr. Dre's dominant release The Chronic album.

It began seeping into MTV's regular video rotation and taking spins away from rock videos. Eventually, MTV began to mix urban music videos in with their regular rotation of mostly rock music, due to the surging popularity of the show "Yo! MTV Raps." Hip

Hop was on the rise creatively, and musically and its influence was growing. 1992 also kicked off what would be later regarded by many as the second Golden Era of hip hop, which lasted until 1996. What does tall of this shit have to do with backpackers now? I'm getting there!

In 1993, Wu Tang Clan (RZA, GZA, Ol Dirty Bastard, Raekwon The Chef, Ghostface Killah, U God, Masta Killa, Inspectah Deck, & Method Man), Boot Camp Click (Black Moon, Smif N Wessun, Heltah Skeltah & O.G.C.), Tha Alkaholiks and the Likwit Crew (King Tee, Lootpack (Madlib, Wildchild & DJ Romes) and Defari), Hieroglyphics Crew (Del The Funkee Homosapien, Souls Of Mischief, Extra Prolific, and Casual), The Beatnuts, Onyx, E-40, Snoop Dogg, and The Roots all hit the hip hop scene hard. These names are legendary in the hip hop industry now and are extremely influential even to this day. Between 1993 and 1996, A long ass list of seminal hip hop albums and classics were released, so I'll skip around liberally.

In 1994, Notorious B.I.G.'s Ready To Die, Nas's Illmatic, Jeru Tha Damaja's The Sun Rises In The East, O.C.'s Times Up, OutKast's Southernplayalisticadillacmusik, and Bone Thugs N Harmony's Creepin On A Come Up EP were all released. In 1995, Mobb Deep dropped The Infamous, The Dogg Pound dropped Dog Food, Raekwon dropped Only Built 4 Cuban Linx, and GZA dropped Liquid Swords. In 1996, Jay-Z released Reasonable Doubt, while Ghostface Killah's dropped Ironman, Busta Rhymes dropped The Coming, Lil Kim's dropped Hard Core, and The Fugees dropped The Score.

The radio was playing all of these artists' material and their videos were getting burn on MTV and BET. The South wasn't yet represented very well in the mainstream or on the radio. Weirder still, Southern artists were moving more units independently and had been properly using their channels of distribution and marketing quietly for years! A Southern rapper/group could sell

100,000-300,000 by word of mouth, shows, and creating a buzz so large that it locked down whole regions of the country....no videos, little or no radio airplay. The thing was that while hip hop was extremely inventive, ground breaking, and influential to pop culture, it wasn't selling very well. If you examine a list of classic hip hop albums from 1986-1996 and look up review how many units they sold, you'll be shocked like I was. I was shocked to find out that albums like K-Solos classic LP album Tell The World My Name (1990) only sold 81,000+ units! This album had 2 major hits and 3 singles, "Spellbound," "Your Moms Is In My Business," and "Fugitive."

If you continue to check on the sales figures of some of the most lauded and universally loved rap/hip hop albums, you'll be shocked to find out that between 90-95% of them caught a brick (which is why they can be found on blogs all over the internet because they're out of print)! Right around the end of 1996, the industry had to go into a different direction or there would be trouble for the music industry — or so they say.

In 1996, the Telecommunications Act was passed. This allowed larger companies to go and buy independent radio stations and put them under their umbrella. The companies that benefited the most from this were Emmis Communications and Clear Channel. Soon there were chain radio stations in effect across the country. Next, record labels began to trim the fat. Some labels folded, and several acts that were prominent before 1996 either were dropped from their labels or they experienced diminished roles of importance in the industry. Artists such as Large Professor — who was signed by Geffen years before and was seen as a landmark signing at the time...until they realized that he wasn't ever going to move a lot of units... — were shelved. (Large Professor in particular was released him from his deal immediately.) Right around this time, a division in the industry began to happen and by 1997, it would be completed.

The division was mainly between the normally underground/ gutter/grimy and conscious hip hop heads and the artists that rhymed about material wealth and the like. A rift had already formed between artist such as Notorious B.I.G. and members of the Bad Boy camp or associates of B.I.G. and Jeru Tha Damaja, O.G.C., and even Ghostface Killah, Raekwon, and Nas. Jay-Z dropped Reasonable Doubt and made rhyming about wealth, extravagance, and hustling seem so fly that between B.I.G. and Jay Z, they spawned a legion of biters! But none of these biters took into account that Jay-Z and B.I.G. were two of the greatest lyricists of all times, a fact that attributed to the music being so appealing. Instead, these wholesale biters figured that if they name drop fashion labels like Gucci, Versace, Donna Karan, DKNY, etc. and rhyme about selling crack, they I'll would blow up!

On the other side of things, 2Pac, who first burst on the scene with Digital Underground and dropped his first album 2Pacalypse Now in 1992 (check the sales numbers!), had become a veritable superstar in his own right. He dropped Strictly For My N.I.G.G.A.Z in 1993 before being incarcerated, and soon after he was released to he dropped the double album Me Against The World to huge sales and much fanfare. The same went for his next album All Eyez On Me. 2Pac had a serious beef with B.I.G. (a beef that involved factors other than just music...even though he admitted to using it to move more units to some journalists such as Danyel Smith and Dream Hampton). 2Pac was a giant in the industry as was B.I.G., whose sophomore album was set to come out.

The mainstream and hip hop media wrote story after story, feature after feature about the East Coast/West Coast Beef. Sales shot up, media coverage increased; very few people noticed the Willie Lynch theory being put into action and played into it entirely. 2Pac had readied a few projects as well. Looking to get out of his 7-album deal with Death Row early, he recorded non-stop.

Ultimately, one fateful night 2Pac was gunned down before he got the chance to put the finishing touch on his 3-part Makaveli series and his One Nation album that would have finished off his Death Row deal and made him a free agent again. Tensions increased and much animosity was sent towards the Bad Boy camp, especially Puff Daddy and Notorious B.I.G. 2Pacs first Makaveli project dropped posthumously and did huge numbers; it still sells to this day.

By 1997, hip hop labels and execs knew what direction that they had to take to get sales up. Notorious B.I.G. was about to drop his sophomore album Life After Death, and that would set the stage for everything. Until tragedy struck once again. The Notorious B.I.G. was gunned down in California before his album was released. This sent a ripple effect throughout the industry. Notorious B.I.G.'s sophomore album dropped posthumously and did huge numbers. (Do you sense a pattern here, people?) After B.I.G. was murdered, a hurt Puff Daddy threw himself into his work and re-recreated his Hell Up In Harlem project into No Way Out. The No Way Out album was released after some largely successful singles and went on to do huge numbers.

That same year, Jay-Z dropped In My Lifetime Vol.1 With the release of this album, Jay-Z poised to become the next "King of New York". All three aforementioned albums crossed over into mainstream radio. Record labels also discovered that if they signed southern artists, they could make noise in the industry as well. Think for a moment: If you sell 100,000-300,000 units without a video, radio airplay or nationwide distribution, how many units would you move with such media support? No Limit Records, Suave House Records, and later Cash Money Records would change the face of the music industry forever, continuing the legacy that Houston's Rap A Lot Records had laid down.

With the shift in the hip hop industry that happened in 1996 and 1997, the underground became its own separate entity, as opposed to just being a part of the larger hip hop mainstream [NO, INCORRECT USE OF WORD. Regardless, underground music is a branch of the hip hop music family, i.e. diaspora.] Rappers and groups from the underground refused to emulate the jiggy/shiny suit/cash flow/thug/mafioso/hustler image that was blowing up all over the radio at the time. Groups and collectives that were once juggernauts, such as Wu Tang Clan, Boot Camp Clik, and even Bone Thugs N Harmony began to experience a decrease in popularity, in airplay, and video play after releasing their 1997 albums. The industry has had shifted. Two thrones were now vacant, and everyone was rushing to fill them — there were Biggie and Pac imitators everywhere.

At the same time, independent distributors like Fat Beats Records, Sandbox Automatic, and many others began to specialize in putting out independent vinyl releases made by groups that were played on college radio and circulated on underground mixtapes.

Indie labels like Solesides, Stones Throw, Rawkus, Fondle Em, Raw Shack, Bomb Hip Hop, Hydra, and Brick began to release singles that attracted many fans that were turned off by the rap music that was now getting spins on the radio ca. 1997/1998. These indie labels began to utilize the internet to sell this underground music and make it possible to listen to it all over the world. Heads would log on to 88HipHop.com, Duckdown. com, Rawkus.com, HipHopSite.com, UndergroundHipHop.com, and SandboxAutomatic.com to hear the latest J Live, Company Flow, Hieroglyphics, Sir Menelik, Mos Def, and Latryx joints that they couldn't hear on the radio or purchase the music that they did hear on college radio but didn't have a place to buy it. the backpacker was born.

By 1998, Def Jam had found the formula to make hits again and released projects by DMX, Ja Rule, Method Man, Redman, and Jay-Z — all albums made serious noise. Along with the rosters at Cash Money Records, No Limit Records, Roc A Fella Records, and Lauryn Hills debut solo album The Miseducation Of Lauryn Hill, rap music had made big inroads into pop culture. And once Def Jam sent the Survival Of The Illest and Hard Knock Life Tours out on the road (and note, they were highly successful and without any incidents of violence in small and large venues), the stage was set. This occurrence opened the floodgates for major hip hop tours to play to huge arenas again. This also put the nail in the coffin for the underground to ever join the hainstream rap scene again. A hip hop Civil War has been going on ever since.

If you were born after the late '70s or the early '80s, you might possibly consider Lupe Fiasco to be a "backpacker"/"backpack rapper". Given the context, this term can be used as an adjective or a derogatory term. But it makes me laugh, really, because none of the people who use this term realize that its it was all basically the product of a perfectly executed plan to remove the creativity, lyricism, fun, and consciousness from mainstream rap. The Willie Lynch theory was once again put into effect. Conscious vs. Material. Hustlers vs. Emcees. Underground vs. Mainstream. Crunk vs. Hyphy. Reggaeton vs. Grime. Old vs. Young....Yes, indeed.

Part 2
RETROSPECTIVES/ PROFILES/REVIEWS

My J Dilla Journey:
A Tale Of Two Jay Dee's; 10 Years Of Fandom vs. 10 Years Of Being A Dilla Scholar (1996-2016)

In February 1996, I first became aware of how great a producer Jay Dee was. A decade later, he passed away at the age of 32. In the decade that followed he became an icon, a cult figure and a target.

In January 1996, I left my home in Boston to attend Morgan State University in Baltimore, MD. At that time, the DMV was going through a kind of mini rap renaissance. Questionmark Asylum had a major label deal. Nonchalant had a song called "5 O'Clock", which eventually became a #1 rap hit (her DJ was Young Guru), and an infamous battle rapper from Richmond, VA named Mad Skillz signed with a major, and released his debut album that February. It was a big deal on campus since so many Virginians went to Morgan State. I'd listen to Morgan State's radio stations WEAA (88.9 FM), WERQ AKA 92Q (92.3 FM), WKYS (93.9 FM) & WPGC (95.3 FM); all played rap and R&B. These stations would compete with each other to be the first to play the hottest music. This made listening to the radio an adventure, and I have to say it was the best regional radio I'd ever experienced firsthand in my life.

That same February, I began to notice that on most of the stations, they would play multiple songs by The Pharcyde in a block and then transition right into edited album tracks from Mad Skillz's album From Where???. After a couple of days, I decided to get to the bottom of it. so I asked my roommate if he had The Pharcyde's album Labcabincalifornia on tape. "You lunchin', Jo! I got that jon' on CD. If the tape popped? That would blow me,

Yung!" was his response. He handed me the CD and I noticed that the songs the radio always played "Runnin'," "Drop," and "Y?," were either produced or co-produced by a dude named Jay Dee. Actually, the radio would play a "Y?" remix as opposed to the original version, so I went throughout O'Connell Hall asking if anyone had the "Y?" single so I could see the credits. I was told that it was actually the B side of the "Drop" single, and somebody brought it down to me in the lobby. On vinyl. There it was again staring me in the face: "Y? (Be Like That)" Jay Dee remix.

The first half of the mystery was over, so I went to the 3rd floor to another cat's room and asked him if he had the Mad Skillz tape. He looked at me as if I asked him if Ananda Lewis was ugly or not. He handed me the tape and I unfolded the J card to read the album credits. That song "The Jam", that the radio stations had played off the album, was also produced by Jay Dee, and so was that other jawn "It's Goin' Down." I'd figured it out, all of those dope ass songs with the ill beats that multiple radio stations were playing in different orders were all made by the same producer. That's crazy! My boy Rashad pointed out to me that Jay Dee also did a remix of Busta Rhymes' "Woo Hah!!". The next month, I noticed he that Jay Dee had contributed to two of the tracks on Busta's debut album The Coming. The songs were "Still Shining" and "Keep It Moving," which Jay Dee had produced as part of The Ummah, the music production collective, composed of Q-Tip and Ali Shaheed Muhammad of A Tribe Called Quest and Jay Dee.

Later on in the school year, De La Soul dropped "Stakes Is High," the lead single from their upcoming album of the same name. The beat was easily one of the best I'd heard in recent memory, making it completely unavoidable the entire summer. Guess who produced it? Jay Dee. I went back to Boston for good about a month later. Once I got home, I had my first of what would be many discussions about Jay Dee with my younger producer brother and my old rhyme partner turned producer Karif who made beats under the name Vanguard. I was briefed on The Ummah and reminded that they produced "1nce Again," the lead single from A Tribe Called Quest's Beats, Rhymes & Life album. However, when the "Stressed Out" single dropped, both album versions were credited to Jay Dee. In addition, Jay Dee had also produced the incredible remix to "She Said" for The Pharcyde. It was then broken down to me how insane his beats — and this lesson was given to me by two cats who had studied producers and music constantly. I was completely receptive because, at this point of my, life I'd finally given up my hoop dreams and could focus on my first love again.

Over the next few years, it was impossible to be around a group of knowledgeable hip hop heads, DJ's, or producers who weren't aware of who Jay Dee of The Ummah was. Between 1998 and 2000, awareness of him shot through the roof in Rap intelligentsia circles. This was partly due to the circulation of third- to tenth-hand cassette dubs of Slum Village's Fantastic Vol. 1, which was fueled by Questlove mentioning Slum Village in the liner notes of The Roots' album Things Fall Apart. Around the same time, DJ Scratch said that "Jay Dee is the most incredible producer. Only a producer can really appreciate the shit he does on beats. He's sick. Nobody should even try to follow him." When DJ Spinna was asked whose beats does he sweat, he responded with: "Most of the Jay Dee stuff. There's a mystery behind his procedure. He's ill." Mind you, this was in the June/July 2000 issue of Blaze Magazine with Swizz Beats and Mannie Fresh on the cover. Heads knew the real...

By the end of 2000, Jay Dee had contributed production to A Tribe Called Quest's The Love Movement, Q-Tip's Amplified, The Roots' Things Fall Apart, Common's Like Water For Chocolate, Slum Village's Fantastic Vol. 2, Busta Rhymes's Anarchy, D'Angelo's Voodoo, and Erykah Badu's Mama's Gun, among other projects. It was only right that he release some solo material. After copping his beats CD's from Bling47 via Sandbox Automatic for years, Jay Dee AKA J Dilla was finally about to drop his own project, Welcome To Detroit, as part of the BBE Beat Generation series. Even after being a fan of his for 5 years, I was blown away by what I heard.

Dilla's legend continued to grow. He was in that circle of producers that was revered by hip hop heads and musicians alike. This is back before it was even common for cats in this space to utilize the internet, so these discussions often happened face to face even as chain record stores and independent record stores alike began closing down. By 2002, digital cable became the new industry standard as did DSL modems, broadband internet, and cable modems that allowed for people to be on the internet 24/7. Since the normal places music lovers and heads used to meet to discuss music were disappearing, these displaced fans began to gravitate to music websites and message boards. His Dilla's work as part of The Ummah and The Soulquarians was often a topic of discussion during this stretch.

In 2003, J Dilla released the Ruff Draft EP on vinyl, along with the highly anticipated Champion Sound, the classic collaborative LP album with Madlib (as Jaylib). In addition, 48 Hours the album he produced for his group Frank & Dank on MCA, leaked and news got out that he made a solo album for MCA that had also been shelved. Between these three releases, Dilla's legend was cemented among fans of quality rap production and musicians alike.

In 2005, Common teamed up with Kanye West to make his comeback album Be. J Dilla and his fellow Soulquarian James Poyser contributed to the album, which had followed up Common's poorly received 2002 LP effort Electric Circus; an album that featured production mostly from Questlove, James Poyser and Dilla. To this day, it cracks me up how people praise Beats, Rhymes & Life, The Love Movement, and Electric Circus due to Dilla's work on them, when I remember all of the venom people had for those albums when they first came out. (Revisionist history at its finest. Or worst.) Also by this time, there were already downloadable folders of Dilla beats floating around all over the internet, and they were traded freely like baseball cards on music sites, message boards and the earliest rap blogs.

In Fall 2005, the word began to spread that Dilla was in bad health, but no one really knew exactly how bad things were until pictures began to circulate on music sites and message boards after his show in Paris back in November 2005. Once that European tour ended in December 2005 and he returned back to California, we began to learn more details and the news was devastating to fans, producers, and musicians alike. J Dilla was a measuring stick that people used to gauge their own progression and without him, many people would lose a major point of inspiration; even cats who were considered masters or legends would lose someone they considered a peer and a contemporary but also an artist whose output served as impetus to push them to create.

At the top of 2006, we were all told we may lose Dilla. and That was a tough pill to swallow. The rap internet/blogosphere was still in its infancy. MySpace was still hot, YouTube was brand new, and Rapidshare, Megaupload and Zshare were the most popular modes of transferring large files. iPhones didn't exist yet and we were still years away from Soundcloud and Mixcloud. In the 10 years since, I had become a fan of Dilla's. He'd come up with a style, smashed the entire game, then scrapped it and went into a completely new phase like Miles Davis, Stevie Wonder, David Bowie, or and Prince would do had done. Meanwhile, people would still be biting his old shit.

In February 2006, Stones Throw released Donuts on Dilla's 32nd birthday. For the first three days that it was out, people were losing their shit over how groundbreaking it was. Then the news came that J Dilla passed away, and the project suddenly took on a bigger meaning than just a mind-blowing beat tape/instrumental project. It was him saying goodbye. Suddenly, there were hidden messages you could decipher. What once was just a dope beat 72 short hours earlier when you played it, suddenly now had a much larger significance. The only remaining projects still in the loop that we were aware Dilla had been working on were The Shining for BBE and Jay Love Japan, which were both released later in 2006.

By 2007, J Dilla was gone, but in his passing an awareness was brought — primarily brought by his friends, admirers, collaborators and fans who followed his career closely — to his vast and highly influential body of work. Dilla wasn't big on being in the spotlight, talking about himself, or playing the game. He preferred to do the work and make the music. However, he had a great deal of people in his corner to present his case to the rest of the world. There was a new wave of young music fans who had just discovered J Dilla and who Dabrye, Spacek, Karriem Riggins, James Poyser, Pino Palladino and Sa-Ra Creative Partners were. The Dilla "Changed My Life" t-shirts gained popularity, as those who had recently become aware of the burgeoning LA beat scene (which sprang up from Low End Theory following the release of Flying Lotus's 1983 EP) discovered Dilla. All of these young but enthusiastic new fans melded with some hyper-vocal zealots who combined to turn a lot of people off, people who were just discovering who Dilla, from exploring his back catalog any further. And lacking people that who are knowledgeable about not only music, but also sample sources and extensive experience in the beatmaking process, meant that a lot of Dilla's genius was lost on these new fans.

I became a blogger in January 2007, but I'd been active on numerous sites and message boards like Okayplayer, Dissensus (UK), AllHipHop, XXL.com, and others before then. I was around for the rise of the LA beat culture as well as the global beat culture between 2006 and 2009. Back then, people went from uploading folders of beats in ZIP or RAR files directly to Rapidshare, Megaupload, MediaFire or Zshare then posting download links on Blogger, Wordpress, or Tumblr to implementing Soundcloud, Mixcloud, or Bandcamp and using Twitter to spread the word. This was when Flying Lotus, Heralds Of Change EP's or anything by Klipm0de Sound Agency was the hottest shit out. During this period, both YouTube and Vimeo became useful for making beat videos or spreading live show footage as beat battles were super popular thanks in part to the Red Bull Big Tune Beat Battle which exploded onto the scene in 2007. All of these things were directly connected to a community of beatmakers and producers who were Dilla fans or inspired by him and who were either fans of beat culture producers, Red Bull Big Tune competitors or both. Alpha Pup and All City releases were prominent. Footage of Low End Theory or Beat Cinema events were posted online. Soundcloud gained more and more of an audience and lots of producers and listeners flocked to Bandcamp. It was during this era that I was listening to a lot of exciting innovation and growth alongside a gang of Dilla clones running with one of his many old styles.

Throughout my years covering the beat culture and the evolution of music production down to beat tapes and instrumental albums, it wasn't lost on any of us how influential Dilla was and how even years after he passed on his presence still loomed large. Some music journalists began to call the entire beat culture "post-Dilla" even though the earliest influences of Low End Theory traced back to 2003 to an event called Sketchbook, so that tag wouldn't be entirely accurate. Soon, J Dilla became the de facto father of the entire beat culture in a similar fashion to how Dana White insists Bruce Lee is the father of MMA even though martial artists and fight historians dispute his claims and repeatedly cite others who combined fighting systems and advocated full contact before Bruce Lee founded Jeet Kune Do in 1967. It's a runaway train now...

To me, James Dewitt Yancey (AKA Jay Dee AKA J Dilla) is easily the most influential producer of the past generation. If you were to ask producers who you think are more influential over this same period (such as Pharrell Williams) for their thoughts on the subject, I'm sure his their responses would be an eye opener. I've had discussions with music journalists, musicians of all backgrounds and disciplines, music producers of numerous genres, and straight up knowledgeable fans that I had very little in common with, but we all spoke Dilla. I grew up in a neighborhood rich in Jazz history, a neighborhood in close proximity to the Boston Conservatory, New England Conservatory of Music, and Berklee College Of Music. So I've been surrounded by music since the womb. Talking music is what I do…I've had so many different kinds of Dilla discussions over the past 20 years. But before I jump down the throat of someone who just discovered his music and or just recently became enamored with it, I instantly think back to February 1996 when I had my lightbulb moment and discovered who was behind that music that made my face scrunch up when I heard it on the radio back when I was 20 going on 21.

Here I am now, more than twenty years after I began my Dilla journey, still in awe that someone who passed away more than a decade ago is still 5 years ahead of the game. Rest in eternal peace, Jay Dee AKA J Dilla.

From Unsigned Hype
To King Of New York:
The Improbable Rise of The
Notorious B.I.G.

In the March 1992 issue of The Source magazine, Matty C (then the man in charge of the Source's "Unsigned Hype" column) picked a demo tape from a Brooklyn cat named Biggie Smalls. The demo was of straight up gutter street rap that included looped up beats with cuts by DJ 50 Grand. It didn't even contain any fully structured songs, but that raw demo tape was still easily head and shoulders above anything else that was submitted to Matty C at the time.

Story goes that anyone else that heard this same demo tape was instantly floored by Biggie's presence, flow, voice, rhymes, and delivery. Hip-Hop was just coming out of an era where Pop Rap was overly dominant and gimmicks and image were important. Biggie didn't dance. Biggie wasn't handsome ("Heartthrob? Never"). Biggie was just immensely talented, so much so that he was undeniable from the first listen. Over the next 5 years this underground rapper from Bedford-Stuyvesant ("Bed Stuy"), Brooklyn would have the most dominant run of any rapper in hip hop history during one of its most competitive eras.

From his first guest appearance on Heavy D's posse track "A Buncha N*ggas" to his first single "Party & Bullshit" (from the Who's The Man soundtrack) and his guest appearances to follow, BIG's verses managed to even set him apart from the rest of the growing number of supremely talented rappers of the era which included Treach, Nas, Jay-Z, Big L, Raekwon, to Ghostface Killah, and Snoop (Doggy) Dogg.

71

In each of hip hop's golden eras, there was a new influx of sonic and lyrical innovators that ultimately created an ultra competitive environment that leads to great music being churned out regularly. Biggie Smalls began as one of those innovators back at the outset of this new era in 1992. And by the time it was all over and the smoke had cleared, he was crowned the undisputed King Of New York.

Big listened to Dr. Dre's The Chronic and Wu Tang Clan's Enter The 36 Chambers and knew where he had to go thematically and sonically with his debut album. He was going to speak to that man or woman who was struggling with day to day life in the inner city, and he was going to strike a chord with them and make music that reflected his experiences simultaneously. Biggie went into the lab with all of these things in mind as he crafted his bars for his debut album, Ready To Die (which was originally going to be released on MCA Records until Sean Combs was fired and released it on his then-upstart record label Bad Boy Records).

Sean "Puffy" Combs landed a situation with Arista Records for his burgeoning label Bad Boy Records. Notorious B.I.G.'s (as Biggie was now formally known as, thanks to the Biggie Smalls pseudonym already being taken) album was highly anticipated after the radio airplay and charts success of the lead single "Juicy" and the buzz his mixtape bars created; and the streets were on fire because of the DJ Premier produced B-side record "Unbelieveable."

Ready To Die was released in September 1994, about 5 months after Nas dropped his damn near perfect classic debut Illmatic on Columbia Records. Keep in mind that Nas was essentially touted as the lyrical reincarnation of Rakim by The Source at the time. They did a cover story about the making of Nas' album, and it even received the coveted 5 mic rating in The Source. By comparison, Ready To Die got 4.5 mics in The Source. But then the streets had their say in the matter.

The Notorious B.I.G. singles "Juicy," "Big Poppa," and "One More Chance," far surpassed Nas's "It Ain't Hard To Tell," "The World Is Yours," and "One Love" in street buzz, radio airplay, and sales numbers. When Ready To Die hit store shelves, it instantly captured the imagination and attention of not only hardcore hip hop heads but it also managed to crossover and eventually win the hearts and minds of casual rap fans as well. Biggie's grimy street tales even resonated with those who resided in the suburbs. In the end, Ready To Die became for the East Coast and New York what Dr. Dre's The Chronic was for the West Coast and Los Angeles.

Biggie's sheer lyrical brilliance and street credibility, coupled with his overwhelming commercial success (thanks to Sean "Puffy" Combs in his role as executive producer, general counsel, and overseer) aided in his improbable ascent to the throne. Christopher Wallace, not Francis M.H. White, had now assumed the mantle of King Of New York all off of one album. And this all achieved at the very same time that Nas and Wu Tang Clan were hotter than volcanic lava.

Big was so ahead of the game that if you pay attention he and Puff shout out the Junior Mafia crew on "Juicy". At the time he began mentioning them on record, they were in the studio unaware he was referring to them. BIG told them, "You're Junior Mafia! You're going to be my crew." The ambitious entrepreneur would soon branch out with Un Rivera, secure a deal for their joint label Undeas, then make and release Junior M.A.F.I.A's "Conspiracy" album.

Undisputed classic rap albums like Mobb Deep's The Infamous and Raekwon The Chef's Only Built 4 Cuban Linx were blaring out of cars from Pasadena to Medina at the time, but none of that stopped The Notorious B.I.G. from completely sweeping the 1995 Source Awards. Ready To Die was still moving units. Conspiracy was moving units. Biggie was on top of the mountain when his competition was the stiffest it had been since Rakim, Big Daddy

Kane, Kool G. Rap, KRS One, Ice Cube, etc. were all at their peaks (circa ca. 1989); and the inevitable backlash had just begun.

Biggie started out as the quintessential hardcore, grimy, raw, backpack rapper. His songs and verses circulated around on mixtapes (even though Dream Hampton told me via Twitter that BIG didn't "get" mixtapes and felt that they were stealing from him) between 1992 and 1994 up until his album dropped, which helped to spread his legend. After he began to experience success and overshadow his talented contemporaries and peers, a mini backlash had set in, one example: "Shark Niggas" on Raekwon The Chef's Only Built For Cuban Linx.

Once Ready To Die exploded and BIG began to appear on every third radio hit — as Bad Boy Records began to dominate the entire urban music landscape with its influence — the backlash suddenly kicked into overdrive. What followed soon afterwards were shots and things that could be perceived or misconstrued as shots that came from artists like De La Soul, Jeru The Damaja, O.G.C., and The Roots in either their rap bars, songs or their music videos.

At that particular time, most of these acts were perceived to be at the opposite end of the hip hop spectrum in 1996. Biggie suddenly went from one of "us" in the army jacket, jeans, and Timberland boots to the dude in the Versace shades who rapped on those damned Total and 112 songs that got played on the radio 30 times a day. He indirectly became the guy responsible/or unfairly blamed for all that "Jiggy shit" you couldn't escape in late 90's urban music, since everyone copied everything Bad Boy did at the time.

The whole playa/Big Willie/Don image that Sean "Puffy" Combs had created for The Notorious B.I.G. had caught on a little too well. Soon, even R&B artists were emulating it. Before long, all of urban music fell under B.I.G.'s influence, and if you were an underground cat or a backpacker you peeped game and your first instinct would be to address it. That being the case, we STILL all acknowledged that Biggie was the nicest cat in the game. Even in a Coogi sweater, Versace shades and gators as opposed to smoking a blunt in an army jacket, black jeans and some Timberlands.

We tend to forget exactly how tumultuous and ultra competitive the rap game was circa 1996. The underground was still part of the fabric of mainstream rap music, but the industry was slowly pulling apart at its seams. The dispute that began between Suge Knight and his vendetta against Bad Boy Records turned into a supposed East Coast/West Coast feud, as evidenced by 2Pac's disses to Biggie, The Dogg Pound's 1995 song and video for "New York, New York," and the Capone-N-Noreaga response record "LA, LA" featuring Mobb Deep & Tragedy Khadafi in early 1996.

As someone who read a dog eared New York Times with the Death Row Records roster on the cover back in January 1996 as a 20 year old freshman at Morgan State University in Baltimore, I can attest to this. Fist fights would break out in my dorm when one person played Biggie and the next room over immediately blasted 2Pac and vice versa. In addition to that, the underground rapper was slowly losing his place in the increasingly jiggy mainstream rap world, and that created a different kind of friction. In September 1996, 2Pac was gunned down at the age of 25 in Las Vegas. Hip hop had suffered the first of several wounds that it would never fully recover from.

Biggie's debut single from his sophomore album Life After Death was officially released on December 13, 1996, exactly 3 months after 2Pac's passing. "Hypnotize" was already a hit on the radio before it was even available commercially. There wasn't a place you could go without hearing it blaring out of speakers. At the same time, the push for Life After Death began in January 1997. The Shiny Suit/Jiggy Era was in full swing. Puff Daddy & Mase's "Can't Nobody Hold Me Down" and Notorious B.I.G.'s "Hypnotize" were #1 & #2 on the Billboard charts before

"Hypnotize" finally took the top spot.

When Biggie was gunned down on March 9, 1997, he was about to take the entire world over. His album Life After Death was about to drop on March 25. Puff Daddy & The Family's Hell Up In Harlem album was waiting in the wings with an #1 single and several guest spots from Biggie on potential hit singles. He was the central figure in the Bad Boy empire and he had laid out a plan to bring forth a supergroup called The Commission featuring himself, Jay-Z, Lil' Cease, and Charli Baltimore (Wu Gambinos and The Firm, I'm looking at you). He was looking into breaking into television and film, plus he had a clothing company on the way called Brooklyn Mint.

The passing of Christopher Wallace is one that hits me hard personally for several reasons. First, due to what's happened with the music industry since Biggie's passing, we will never again have an underground raw street rapper emerge, minus the hype based on his pure talent alone, get signed to a major label, make his way through the ultra competitive underground, then move into the even more competitive mainstream rap world during a golden era of emceeing.

Not only that, but through his talent, creativity and lyricism alone he dominated an era that was loaded to the gills with greats and legends. There wasn't any hype with Big, it was all earned. No asterisks will go next to his name in the hip hop history books. The same way you go and ask some great producers who the best was and they constantly answer with "Dilla" it's the exact same way with Biggie. If you try that, "He only had two albums" argument with me as to why he shouldn't be considered in the discussion for the greatest rapper, that just proves that you didn't fully experience or grasp the years of 1992-1997 in hip hop.

RIP Christopher "Notorious B.I.G." Wallace. The rap game never fully recovered from your loss.

GZA's *Liquid Swords*:
A 20th Anniversary Retrospective

When the Wu Tang Clan was formed in 1992, it was a direct result of the bad experiences both RZA (formerly Prince Rakeem) and GZA (formerly The Genius) accumulated while being signed to record label deals in 1991. While Prince Rakeem only released an EP on Tommy Boy, The Genius released a full length LP "Words From The Genius," which received nearly no push from Cold Chillin'/Warner Bros. By 1992, RZA and GZA were done with their obligations to their former labels, but they developed an idea that would yield Wu-Tang Clan's debut 12" single, "Protect Ya Neck"/ "Method Man." The next year, the Wu-Tang Clan released their 1st first album on Loud/RCA which kicked off their new careers as members of a group/collective.

Beginning in November, 1994, the first of the RZA orchestrated Wu-Tang Clan solo albums were released. First was Method Man's "Tical," followed by Old Dirty Bastard's "Return To The 36 Chambers: The Dirty Version," which was released in late March, 1995; then came Raekwon's "Only Built 4 Cuban Linx…" in early August 1995. Each album became progressively better and was better received than the previous project. The Wu were on a roll and next up to the plate was GZA, who had the advantage of experience, plus he had been present for the creation of the preceding solo Wu albums. He toiled meticulously on trying to take the cinematic approach Raekwon & Ghostface employed but ramping it up to another level.

Both GZA & Raekwon/Ghostface Killah contributed songs/ singles to the original soundtrack of the 1994 film "Fresh," which served as lead singles for their upcoming projects. For Rae & Ghost that was "Heaven & Hell" and for GZA it was "I Gotcha' Back."

GZA threw himself into writing and recording his forthcoming opus and building with RZA in his basement studio, where the bulk of the first round of Wu-Tang solo projects were crafted. GZA recorded his verses over and over again and carefully constructed them over time until the rhymes and production matched the urgency and intensity of a film noir suspense/thriller or a crime film. The dark, somber, heavily detailed, layered super visual aesthetic he wanted to replicate was crucial to relay to the audience, as the listener had to suspend disbelief as if they were watching a movie as opposed to just listening to an album.

On October 10, 1995 GZA released the single "Liquid Swords" on to an unsuspecting populace. (It was the same day AZ released his debut album, Doe Or Die.) The song immediately caught on with audiences. It got steady radio play and the video entered the rotation on both MTV and BET. This was crucial, as MTV had done away with "Yo! MTV Raps" a few months earlier in August, 1995. so This meant that GZA's "Liquid Swords" video was being played in the regular rotation right alongside Smashing Pumpkins, No Doubt, Bush, Silverchair, Goo Goo Dolls, Alanis Morrisette, Red Hot Chili Peppers, Oasis, Mariah Carey, Whitney Houston, and the latest Michael Jackson videos.

Due to the haunting, eerie sounds of the single and the fact that the video was played alongside the popular rock and alternative hits of the time, it soon gained favor with that same audience. This resulted in "Liquid Swords" cracking the Billboard Hot 100 and climbing high enough that it entered the Top 50, ultimately peaking at #48. That was certainly a surprise. And it went Top 5 on the Billboard Hot Rap charts, peaking at #3.

Liquid Swords, the album, was released on November 7, 1995. On that same day Erick Sermon's Double Or Nothing and Goodie Mob's Soul Food also dropped. Two weeks earlier, Onyx had released their sophomore effort All We Got Iz Us. A week after that, The Pharcyde dropped their second album

Labcabincalifornia. And a week after this, LL Cool J dropped "Mr. Smith" (an album which for LL represented another successful comeback). Other albums released during this stretch include: Mic Geronimo's The Natural, Fat Joe's Jealous Ones Envy, and Funkmaster Flex 60 Minutes Of Funk—The Mixtape Vol. 1. I point all of these releases out to provide context for those who weren't privileged enough to be of record-buying age at the time. Also, I do it to let provide more context about what the landscape looked like at the time GZA's album first hit the market so that you can better understand its reception. Given the recent wave of online "Rap writers" who feel it's a good idea to try to downplay the classic rap releases of the 90's, they're actually simultaneously revealing how little they know about the period.

The psychology of the audience/listener directly relates to the art they consume at the time they ingest it. In November, the days suddenly got darker way sooner following Daylight Savings Time (which switched back on October 29, 1995) as the Fall season slowly transitioned into Winter. On November 28th, GZA released the Inspectah Deck guested single "Cold World."

The ominous sounding single would steadily ascend the Rap charts and crack the Top 10 (peaking at #8), enter the R&B charts (peaking at #57), and surprisingly even sneak its way onto the Billboard Hot 100 before stalling at #97. The single's life was no doubt extended by a brilliant remix featuring D'Angelo, which gained serious legs on the mixtape circuit, mixshows, and college radio.

Both November and December 1995 were rather cold and January 1996 opened up with a huge blizzard all up and down the Eastern Seaboard. This provided the perfect storm (pun unintended) for Liquid Swords to gain traction with music fans organically. As the weather got progressively colder, it seemed like more and more people began to gravitate to Liquid Swords. This isn't based on sales number provided by Soundscan via a Google search, this was my personal experience from that same time period. I remember this album being the unofficial soundtrack to the entire 1995/96 holiday season.

I traveled to Morgan State University in Baltimore (MD) during that same blizzard just to spend a close to a week snowed in at my new home, O'Connell Hall. That dorm housed athletes, freshmen, and thugs (seriously) from New York, Massachusetts, New Jersey, Connecticut, Pennsylvania (mainly Philadelphia & Pittsburgh), Delaware, Maryland, Virginia, D.C., and all over California. One thing they all had in common (even when they beefed over Tupac and Biggie) was that they all played GZA's Liquid Swords throughout those cold ass months.

Liquid Swords became the official soundtrack of Winter 1995/96 and has become one of the greatest Winter albums ever made, due in large part to the early commitment RZA and GZA made to constructing such a dense, haunting project. In January 1996, the RIAA awarded GZA with a plaque denoting his album topped sales in excess of 500,000 units to go Gold.

In March 1996, I remember GZA's split video for "Shadowboxin'"/"4th Chamber" becoming the Hip Hop Pick on BET's "Rap City." It made perfect sense that RZA and GZA were able to collaborate on such a cinematic project, seeing as how they were both accomplished directors themselves. Their eyes for detail and hyperawareness of the importance of visuals was apparent in the graphic design and packaging of the album (a collaboration between GZA and comic book artist Denys Cowan) and the fact GZA directed all of the videos for Liquid Swords.

I have rarely seen an artist execute an album to this level until Kanye West had control of not only his creative process, production and visuals in the early to mid-00's. Most recently, I was reminded of Liquid Swords by KA's self-produced 2012 magnum opus Grief Pedigree. where he also directed videos for each song. A testament to the timelessness of Liquid Swords is the fact that it finally went

Platinum in 2015, almost 20 years after it initially went Gold. I saw GZA perform this album in its entirety with a live band three years ago and it just solidified exactly how concise of a project it was. No matter how many years removed we are from its initial release, it still sounds as raw and gritty as it did when it was first taken out of the shrink-wrapped plastic and inserted into either the box, Walkman, or CD player.

Even to this very day, whenever I hear "Duel Of The Iron Mic", "Killah Hills 10304" or "Swordsman," I'm instantly transported back to those frigid nights playing this cassette in my Walkman. I remember those excursions in cars with Liquid Swords playing in the CD player, plus all of those days and nights playing Super Nintendo, PlayStation and Sega Saturn in dorm rooms all over Morgan State University with "B.I.B.L.E (Basic Instructions Before Leaving Earth)" blaring out of speakers.

"Fight The Power":
The Full Story Behind One of
Rap's Most Iconic Songs

In late September, 1988, just after finishing nine weeks of shooting his third feature film, *Do The Right Thing*, Spike Lee had the first of several conversations with Public Enemy & The Bomb Squad about them contributing a song for it. Spike Lee's initial idea was for Public Enemy to make an updated version of the old Negro National Anthem "Lift Ev'ry Voice And Sing" with Terrence Blanchard, but Public Enemy convinced Lee that they needed to take another approach, and he left them to the job.

Inspired by The Isley Brothers' 1975 single "Fight The Power (Pts. 1 & 2)," from their landmark LP , *The Heat Is On,* The Bomb Squad went to work creating an anthem that would come to define the Summer of 1989 the same way that The Isley Brothers' opus did the Summer of 1975. After it was completed and submitted to Spike Lee, the group was surprised at how often he used it in the film. It was the film's heartbeat, its recurring theme, and it would no doubt be the song that would define the soundtrack released by Motown just before the film was released in theaters.

On April 22nd, 1989, in the Bedford-Stuyvesant neighborhood of Brooklyn, where *Do The Right Thing* was shot the previous Summer, Spike Lee directed Public Enemy's music video for "Fight The Power," which doubled as a youth march through the streets of Brooklyn. Spike Lee had high hopes for this song as the backbone of his film; and Motown was banking on this song to help push the film's soundtrack to a younger and wider audience. Def Jam also had high hopes, as the label was banking on Public Enemy's next single to be a hit to create momentum for their upcoming album (the group's third), which was still in its planning stages. On May 19th, 1989, Spike Lee screened *Do The Right Thing* at the Cannes Film Festival, and the film was to enter limited theatrical release in North American theaters on June 30th, 1989. While the film made the majority of the jury nervous at Cannes (except for Sally Field who loved it), all Spike needed to do was avoid any controversy that could hurt the film.

On May 22nd, 1989, an interview ran in the Washington Times that contained several ant-Semitic statements by Public Enemy member Professor Griff, who had been previously censured by the group on multiple occasions for similar infractions. Things came to a head on June 20th, 1989, when journalist R.J. Smith addressed Public Enemy's reluctance and inability to punish Professor Griff for his latest transgression ("The Enemy Within," *Village Voice*). Not coincidentally, that was the same day that the soundtrack for *Do The Right Thing* was released containing Public Enemy's song "Fight The Power," and it was 10 days before the film began its run in selected theatres and arthouses nationwide. Def Jam, Rush Artist Management, and Public Enemy had to address this issue to avoid a backlash that could not only hurt the film but potentially end their careers as recording artists.

On June 21st, 1989, Public Enemy held a press conference where they announced that Professor Griff was no longer a member of Public Enemy. This was followed by a joint statement issued by Public Enemy, Def Jam, and Rush Artist Management which stated that Public Enemy was "disbanding for an indefinite period of time." That Friday, Chuck D appeared on MTV's "This Week In Rock" with Kurt Loder and said the group was pretty much over due to many disagreements amongst members and their handlers over the best way to address the situation with Professor Griff.

Due to the controversy, Def Jam had halted them from going forth with their follow up album to *It Takes A Nation Of Millions…*"

The date was June 23rd, 1989, one week before *Do The Right Thing* was set to begin its limited run in slightly over 350 theaters in North America.

To make matters more confusing, Public Enemy was, for all intents and purposes, disbanded at the time *Do The Right Thing* debuted in theaters. Some theaters were picketed by members of the Jewish Defense Organization who were extremely vocal in calling for the boycott of the film due to the usage of Public Enemy's "Fight The Power" in it. They even distributed leaflets that included a timeline of previous infractions, the group's association with the Hon. Minister Louis Farrakhan of The Nation Of Islam, and critiques from *New York Magazine* that characterized the film as "dangerous."

Public Enemy, while not officially a group were set to have the 7" and cassingle of "Fight The Power" be released on July 4th, 1989 and the following week on July 11th, 1989 Public Enemy's tour VHS "Fight The Power Live" (which contained a promo for the film *Do The Right Thing*) would hit store shelves 10 days ahead of the film's wide release in theaters. It was essentially a waiting game to see how the film and song "Fight The Power" would both be received by the general public.

On July 8th, 1989, in his *Billboard* column "The Rhythm And The Blues," Nelson George wrote a treatise titled "Rap Act Featured In Controversial Lee Film Breaks Up: Did Public Enemy Do The Right Thing?." In it, he detailed the timeline that led to the group disbanding while discussing the song "Fight The Power" and its importance to the film. Incidentally, the soundtrack entered the Top Black Albums chart that week at #84, and "Fight The Power" not only entered at #81 on the Hot Black Singles charts, it also was listed as the #1 Breakout Song on the Hot Dance Music Sales charts before the full numbers for the week were even in. This is something that was no longer allowed in *Billboard* by 1995.

The next week when the sales numbers were finally tabulated?

"Fight The Power" leaped to #66 on the Hot Black Singles chart, entered the Hot Dance Music 12" inch sales chart at #31, and entered Hot Rap Singles chart at #8. That marks the highest debut by a Rap single since Tone Loc's "Funky Cold Medina" that April. Not only that but the video for "Fight The Power" was playing on multiple video shows on BET and was airing on MTV. For a group that had disbanded, it seemed that Public Enemy had the makings of a hit on their hands.

By July 15th,1989, Spike Lee's *Do The Right Thing* was a critical and a financial success already. It had already managed to gross over twice its $6.5 million dollar budget in only its third week of limited release. That's an impressive feat considering it was on less than 500 screens while *Batman* was on 2201 and *Ghostbusters II* was on 1978 that same week. The controversy hadn't been a deterrent; instead, the song had helped to galvanize audiences and made people want to see the film by the time it finally went into wide release on July 21st, 1989. The popularity of "Fight The Power" only grew with the passage of time.

While "Fight The Power" was moving units there were a few crucial factors which prevented it from ultimately going Gold and Platinum. For one, with most other Def Jam singles, there was the song then the instrumental — unless it was a single or double-sided single released after the album was released. This meant that fans would visit the record store in droves and seek out the instrumental for "Fight The Power," especially after hearing Radio Raheem play what seemed to be the instrumental all throughout the film. Brandford Marsalis' contribution was a huge selling point. However, people were disappointed to discover that on the B side there was no instrumental to be found. Instead, the Motown single offered "Flavor Flav Meets Spike Lee," where Spike Lee and Flavor Flav had an almost 5 minute long conversation/argument over the beat. If there had been an instrumental in it's stead, there's no doubt the single would've topped a million copies sold.

Even without an instrumental on the flip side, "Fight The Power" hit #1 on the Hot Rap Singles and stayed there for 6 consecutive weeks between July 29th and September 2nd, 1989. On Wednesday, August 9th, 1989, exactly 8 weeks from their initial press conference and statement, Public Enemy released a new statement announcing that Public Enemy, sans Professor Griff, was "back in action", and not only that but Def Jam and Rush Artist Management added that Public Enemy's third album, *Fear Of A Black Planet*, was back on and expected to be released sometime in the coming Winter. Not a moment too soon, exactly two weeks after Public Enemy announced their return, 16-year old Yusef Hawkins was killed in the Brooklyn neighborhood of Bensonhurst. Public Enemy's "Fight The Power" was often played in the many subsequent protest marches led by Rev. Al Sharpton.

In addition, on September 4th, 1989, in Virginia Beach, VA thousands of HBCU students clashed with overaggressive and hostile police during the second day of Greekfest. After being constantly harassed, monitored, and racially profiled several visitors complained about their treatment but it all fell on deaf ears. Thousands of fed up students took to Atlantic Avenue, the Virgina Beach Police called in the National Guard. Donning riot gear, they used force to clear the streets. Rioting ensued and as the youth confronted the advancing forces, they chanted "Fight the power."

Wherever there was unrest and inequality, people were using "Fight the power" as a rallying cry. To further hammer things home, Public Enemy's home VHS release, "Fight The Power Live," was a top selling video that was certified Gold on September 22nd, 1989.

In the end, Chuck D (as Carl Ryder), Hank Shocklee, Keith Shocklee, and Eric "Vietnam" Sadler did exactly what they set out to do by creating an anthem that not only defined the Summer of 1989 but became a classic and one of the most iconic and enduring Rap songs of the past 30 years. And to think, it didn't even go Gold!

How Rawkus' *Soundbombing II* Launched a New Era of Independent Rap

In the summer of 1999, the rap industry was moving into previously unexplored territory. Twenty years after the very first rap 12-inch was released, the genre had finally become the top-selling in terms of sales. Rap was the most popular kind of music amongst the youth and the most sought after demographic from brands and corporations looking to sell products to both Generation X and burgeoning Millennials.

There was a time when rap music couldn't be played on Black radio while the sun was still up. Rap was once relegated to the very back of the record store, partially because it wasn't regarded as real music and partially to discourage shoplifters (since they would essentially have to sprint through the entire store in order to escape with their ill-gotten vinyl, cassette tape, or CD long box.) All of this could be said for mainstream Rap music, but underground/indie Rap in 1999 was perceived much like a red-headed stepchild. It was dismissed as "backpack Rap" where hundreds of lyrical-spiritual-miracle loving "heads" who lived for obscure references, punchlines, metaphors, similes, internal rhyme schemes, multi-syllable rhyme schemes, speed, and remarkable breath control had nerdgasms over vinyl singles that were insanely hard to locate. They existed only to nod their heads furiously to songs with 30 bar verses — no hooks — and thumb their noses at everything on the radio. That was the general consensus.

"Backpacker" was often used as a slur/derogatory term in a world where Swizz Beatz and Mannie Fresh ruled the radio and the charts. Rawkus was the leading brand in underground rap in 1999. Whereas other indie Rap labels made their marks selling

12-inch vinyl singles and CD's through Web-based mail-order marketplaces, such as Sandbox Automatic, Underground Hip-Hop, and Hip-Hop Site, and physical storefronts like Fat Beats. Rawkus did all that and sold a significant amount of CDs. Rawkus had the advantage of being well funded, this meant they had quite a promotional budget. They could secure print ads in all the major and independent music publications. They could afford TV spots, ad space on the radio, and they could shoot videos for their big singles which landed in the rotation on BET, MTV, and MTV2.

On top of it all, Rawkus had Priority/EMI doing their distribution. This allowed Rawkus to compete with major labels in terms of reach. This was something other leading underground Rap labels like Fondle 'Em, Dolo, Stones Throw, Solesides, Hydra, Rhymesayers, and Conception couldn't do. Rawkus had been building up to this point for years. Back in 1997, they had released two seminal projects: Company Flow's *Funcrusher Plus* and the first edition of their compilation series *Soundbombing*. In 1998, Rawkus further established themselves by putting out the double CD compilation *Lyricist Lounge Vol. 1* and the highly anticipated project *Mos Def & Talib Kweli Are Black Star*. They had made such headway that Funkmaster Flex was even playing Rawkus songs on Hot 97. After making several key signings, Rawkus was set to drop multiple projects in 1999, using *Soundbombing II* as the foundation of their releases going forward.

Between their flagship artists who released popular vinyl singles — like Sir Menelik, Shabaam Sahdeeq, RA The Rugged Man, and Talib Kweli & Mos Def — and new signees, like the Cocoa Brovaz (Smif N' Wessun), Da Beatminerz, and The High & Mighty, Rawkus was ready to make a major push that year. The label co-owners Brian Brater and Jarret Myer had funding from James Murdoch (the son of billionaire Rupert Murdoch). They assembled a team that included lead A&R Black Shawn; associate A&Rs Mike Heron and Sally Morita; radio promotions guy Ben

Willis; and Kevin Shand, who did distribution and sales. Gang Starr Foundation's Headqcourterz headed up the Rawkus street team. This outfit was behind one of the most successful stretches an underground Rap label ever achieved.

In addition to having full-page ads in music publications, the video for Common and Sadat X's "1-9-9-9" was in rotation on BET and MTV. Rawkus went a step further by distributing a promotional snippet mixtape by J-Rocc & DJ Babu of the World Famous Beat Junkies. Needless to say, Rawkus' aggressive approach yielded great returns — far beyond what most underground Rap labels experienced.

On May 18th, 1999, *Soundbombing II* hit store shelves. The album was powered by the popularity of "1-9-9-9," Eminem's "Any Man," The High & Mighty's "B-Boy Document 99," and Company Flow's "Patriotism," among other Rawkus songs which were prominently featured on *And1 Mixtape Vol. 1* and *Vol. 2* by DJ Set Free and Nex Millen. There was even a special Rawkus *Soundbombing II* episode of BET's Rap City that aired around the time of the compilations' release. Due to all of these factors, the album did even better than anyone could've wildly anticipated out of the gate.

In the June 5th edition of *Billboard*, *Soundbombing II* not only debuted at #6 on the Top R&B Albums chart, it entered the Billboard 200 at #30. There were multiple Rawkus releases in the Top 10 Rap Singles and there was going to be a *Soundbombing II* series of double-sided vinyl released for their rabid fanbase on five different 12-inches. At the time Rawkus was moving anywhere around 50K units per vinyl drop, occasionally even more. By locking down the crowd on Stretch & Bobbito's WKCR, Jay Smooth's Underground Railroad show on WBAI, DJ Riz and DJ Eclipse on Halftime Radio Show — in addition to Sway, King Tech, and DJ Revolution's The Wake Up Show — they had already secured a faithful core audience who frequented Fat Beats or copped from online marketplaces. But they had made inroads to the wider mainstream rap audience and had converted some of them to the cause of the resistance.

Why was *Soundbombing II* so crucial? Its overwhelming success paved the way for a landmark 1999 for Rawkus. In June, 1999, they released Company Flow's *Little Johnny From The Hospital* and DJ Spinna's *Heavy Beats Vol. 1* which was followed up by The High & Mighty's *Home Field Advantage* in August. These albums set the stage for Rawkus to drop Mos Def's *Black On Both Sides* and Pharoahe Monch's *Internal Affairs* in consecutive weeks in October. These albums helped to raise Rawkus' profile to the point that MTV greenlit a sketch comedy show based on The Lyricist Lounge Show which debuted in early 2000.

Rawkus had become the leading brand carrying the flag for underground Rap as we were deeply entrenched in the Jiggy Era at that point.

Another reason why Rawkus' accomplishments were so timely is because the entire landscape of the music industry was changing. By May, 1999, it was reported that "mp3" was the most searched term on the Internet — ahead of "sex." On May 19th, 1999, it was announced in major business periodicals that MTV was going to purchase The Box meaning that it would join MTV, MTV2, VH1, and BET as Viacom owned music video networks that were portals for urban music. The music industry was scrambling to find ways to regulate music and curb unauthorized downloads of ripped mp3 via sites like MP3.com, MusicMatch and Goodnoise. The industry was trying to create copy-protected CDs or anti-copying protocols for digital music downloads.

Of course, all of this was made moot on June 1st, 1999 when Northeastern University student Shawn Fanning released the beta version of Napster, which spread from Northeastern to Emerson College, Boston University, Berklee College of Music, MIT, Harvard, Boston College and over 50 institutions of higher learning with high-speed Internet in the Metro Boston Area. From there, Napster spread up and down the Eastern Seaboard then nationwide. Nothing would be the same after the Summer of 1999, but with the perfectly timed release of *Soundbombing II*, Rawkus was able to establish itself as a powerhouse right before the inception of the brave new world of P2P sites.

Part 3
PERSONAL ESSAYS

Glorified Bum

Let me rehash my day for you all. First off, it's a holiday so there's no mail. Secondly, I'm watching my nephew for the extended weekend. Third, benefits don't kick in until the 11th and it's the 10th, so I can't shop for food until tomorrow and I'm down to three slices of bread in the loaf. So only the nephew gets the luxury of having toast with his breakfast today. I'm a 36-year-old hip hop blogger. One of the most respected in the world. Just one thing: Critical acclaim and respect doesn't pay the fuckin' bills.

Last week, I agreed to go to a show tonight to write a review of the show. Since then I paid rent, got a birthday gift for my niece, and sold an iPhone 4 to buy an iPhone 4S just for me to discover I can't upgrade MY phone until late November. Right now, I'm using an LG Shine II, which makes people think that either I'm being extremely frugal or I'm a terror suspect. moreso This sentiment is even more apparent when I'm at an event and I'm the only "writer" or blogger there without a business card. Then again, my wallet is just for show. Plus, it looks like it belonged to a dead hobo from the '40's who carried a stick with a kerchief tied to it.

I leave my house and walk to the Green Line MBTA station that will take me to the show I'm supposed to go to. I don't bring money because I have none. Sure, I have a wallet. It has my ID's in it. Also my CharlieCard and the $10 MetroCard I bought when I visited New York back in May. It also holds my PayPal card, which is empty and when I get money in my PayPal account I need to transfer it before I can use it on the card. Don't ask why. In any event, I arrive at the venue to discover that I'm not on the list. Great.

I call my contact and, as would be expected, the act that I'm going to see is hella busy, so they can't be bothered to add someone they don't know to the list. Completely understandable. My contact says something I can't hear over the frolicking youth that reek of marijuana. I ask her what she said and she says, "Just buy a ticket and I'll compensate you via PayPal." That's actually a fair thing to do; problem is I'm completely broke. One of the kids in the line, reeking of the pungent aroma of weed, asks me if I'm Dart Adams. Yep, thar he. I'm a glorified bum that still depends on other people to get into shows I should be able to afford by now.

I had two options left. One, hit up my boy who was opening and try to get him to get me in. Problem was he was actually spinning at the time this was all happening. My second option, call my other boy who was there and ask him to buy my ticket for me (then when I got compensated I'd pay him back). Yeah, no. I instead decided to walk all the way back home from Allston to the South End rather than spend any more money on my CharlieCard. Me and my integrity went for a long leisurely stroll. On the plus side? It's a gorgeous night to stroll along the Boston University campus.

In short, I had a bad night. No one was at fault, shit happens. If anyone is to blame here it's me. Sure, I have a book I still need to finish editing so it drops before the world ends. Sure, I'm still in the process of waiting for a few unfinished projects to actually come to fruition, but there's no excuse why after more than five years of busting my ass writing like a madman (and the year plus I've been doing online radio) that I'm still essentially nowhere. Don't think that'll make me stop doing what I'm doing though. This will just make me work harder so I'm still not in this same exact situation next year. Most bloggers wouldn't dare write any shit like this because it's a bit too real. Fuck 'em. They ain't me.

Dear Mama

I've entered a stage of my life where's there's no manual. Typically, people have their mid-life crisis now, but I had mine between ages 29 and 30, so it's out of the way. I'm three months shy of 42, in a space where age isn't an advantage, while not trying to put real effort into advancing my "career." In real life, I'm in a gray area because I lost my last remaining parent last August due to cervical cancer.

To this day, I field questions about my mom and I still receive her mail. My father passed away 20 years ago, and my grandparents on both sides are no longer alive so that makes my siblings and me the elders in our immediate family. If you still have your parents and grandparents around, cherish the shit out of them. When Thanksgiving comes around and you're the one in the "uncle with the stories" role, as opposed to someone much older than you, it's a real mind fuck to say the least.

Mother's Day is on Sunday and it will be my first one without my mom being here. I survived Thanksgiving, Christmas, and New Year's just fine, but there's another wrinkle. My mom didn't really "get" what I did. I wrote online for years, but she didn't realize that I was a "real" writer until my name appeared on a byline in the Bay State Banner years ago, or it when my name was mentioned in a print article in DigBoston. When anyone mentioned me to her by my pen name, instead of the one she gave me, she was kind of surprised that anyone actually read what I spent hours on without receiving a paycheck. It's really hard to explain to someone born in 1943 — someone who used a slide rule to do math, who wasn't into Sci Fi or fantasy — that many people preferred to use the internet to get their news and entertainment. Or that I use it to gain readership in HOPES of having someone read my work and pay me to write somewhere down the line. She thought I was wasting my time and I needed to get a "real" job. I'm sure when she passed she was worried I wouldn't be able to support myself.

My father was heavy into Sci Fi. He was a computer programmer at one point in time. He bought us a Vic-20, then immediately upgraded to a Commodore 64 back in the early '80s. He'd encourage his kids to program in BASIC or learn another language like COBOL or FORTRAN. He's the one who first showed us Star Wars in a huge metal top-loading VCR and played videogames on his Texas Instruments TI-80/4A home computer.

My mom handled the other stuff. She was the one my younger brother and I used to watch in the kitchen. She was the one who taught me how to do math in my head. My mom used to send me to the numerous dictionaries and encyclopedias we kept on our living room bookshelves to look stuff up when I asked her a question.

Before moving to Boston, my mother was a math teacher in Alabama. When busing happened in Boston back in 1976, it resulted in a lot of school closings. One byproduct was there being a bunch of unused schoolbooks just circulating around the city. My mom gathered a great many of them up, put them on one of the two bookshelves in our old living room, and my siblings and I spent many hours of my youth reading them. After Walter Simonson's Thor comics, my mom introduced me to Norse folktales through her old college copy of Bulfinch's Mythology.

She used to work late at a South End neighborhood drug store called Braddock Drug going back to the early '60s; it was one of the last remaining holdovers from the Jazz Era. Everyone around knew her as Miss Barbara. Thus, I spent most of life as "Miss Barbara's son," until I became known as Dart Adams. As a single mother she raised four kids in Boston's Roxbury and South End neighborhoods between the late '60s and the mid '90s, all of whom managed to go to advanced classes in public school, and then on to

Boston Latin School. Boston Latin School is the oldest and first public school in the United States (1635), a place so prestigious white parents sent their children to parochial and private schools and paid for tutors to prepare them for the infamous "Latin test." This is the same school that prompted the creation of Harvard so its graduates would have a place to go.

None of us ended up drug addicts or did any jail time, which I can't say for many of the other kids who came up in my neighborhood during a stretch that included the Crack Era. There were times we didn't even have electricity or hot water, but my mom found ways to make do, whether it involved heating up hot water on the range or stealing electricity from somewhere using hella extension cords so we could each have space heaters in the winter. We once had a kerosene heater that required my big brother and I to go to a gas station a couple of miles away to get fuel. We took turns carrying it back to our apartment.

Even when we went long stretches without power or lights, my mother wouldn't let us make excuses. My younger brother and I did our homework by candlelight or used flashlights if we needed to. My mother found ways to get us up for school and make sure we did what we were supposed to during those rough years. Even going through all of that, my sister managed to graduate from Wellesley, one of the most prestigious and highly respected institutions of higher education in the country. And my big brother got a scholarship to Northeastern, then later joined the Air Force. For all the sacrifices my mother made for her kids and all the years she worked her fingers to the bone to provide for her children to have better lives, it sucked that I never was able to become successful enough to repay her or take care of her in the manner she deserved.

Two summers ago my mother was receiving chemo and radiation treatments for her cervical cancer. My younger brother and I would take turns bringing her to appointments at the hospital.

After that round of treatments, she wasn't doing too well so she had to be admitted to the hospital again. Things got progressively worse. She was in and out of the hospital until I was told that she had anywhere from weeks to months to live, as the cancer had spread. That was our last hospital visit. A week shy of seven months later, she was gone.

This was last Summer. When my mother died, I didn't post about it on Facebook. I didn't do an Instagram post. I didn't even tweet about it. I didn't cry either. I wanted to cry watching her suffer for over six months straight, but once she finally transitioned and no longer had to go through that pain anymore? I just felt relief. I still haven't cried. Don't know if I ever will, but I do know I had to finally confront my feelings the best way I know how. Through writing.

I was actually trying to take care of her at home until she passed, but ultimately it got to be too much and we opted to put her in hospice care. I wouldn't wish watching your parent deteriorate and be in constant pain on my worst enemy. There wasn't shit I could do but just be there. It was all about pain management and making her transition as comfortable as possible — neither of which I was qualified for. It was bad enough my mother was going to be gone and I still hadn't become anywhere near the success I'd hoped I'd be. It makes sense she'd be concerned about me still pursuing my dreams in my early 40s. But one thing I'm sure she knew was that I would never take the conventional route. Nothing is ever easy for me.

Even though Ma (I called her Ma, actually I'd occasionally call her "Barbara" because I'm the middle child… long fucking story) and I didn't have a lot in common, one thing we did have was our love of the Boston Celtics. This woman loved the Celtics so much you could walk past the TV while someone was shooting free throws and if they missed it'd be your fault. We'd turn to the Celtics game then turn the sound down while turning up the radio so we could hear Johnny Most do color commentary. During the stretch when the Celtics missed the playoffs between 1995 and 2002 was sheer hell. That is, until the 2002 NBA Playoffs, when the Boston Celtics — led by Antoine Walker and Paul Pierce — made an unexpected run to the Eastern Conference Finals. That was the year she began going back to games with my big sister. The Patriots had just won the Super Bowl a few months before, so there was a great deal of excitement around.

Regardless of how differently we saw the world, one thing we could always bond over was the Patriots, Red Sox, and the Celtics. (Ma didn't really love hockey — sorry, Bruins.)

Right now the Boston Celtics are one game away from returning to the Eastern Conference Finals, and they also have a shot to land the #1 pick in the 2017 NBA Draft. It reminds me of 15 years ago when the city was excited about the Celtics again and my mom was yelling at Toine for shooting too many threes and Tony Battie for shooting too many jumpers and not staying in the paint to rebound. Now I find myself watching a bunch of cats with only one legitimate superstar and a deep bench win games by playing team defense, sharing the ball, outworking the other teams and shooting a lot of threes. Ma would have loved it, although I'm sure that she'd be pissed off about the fact that they can't rebound for shit. Only fucks me up more knowing tonight they have a shot to close out the Wizards and she's not going to be here to see it.

My mom had a saying which drove me insane whenever she said it, but as I got older made more and more sense. "A bow knot will untie." It was her way of telling me that even when things seem unlikely or even impossible, they aren't. I was able to survive the toughest times of my life when I was at my absolute lowest by remembering the lessons she taught me and recalling the miracles she pulled off raising her own children. I'm going to be just fine because of the strength, standards, and values she instilled in me.

It does bother me that my mother passed away worried about how I'd be able to support myself in a dying field, knowing that I'm not always big on compromise and I don't really hold my tongue. Anytime I showed her a book I was quoted in, or I was recognized in the street, she'd ask when I was going to be able to monetize or finally break through in writing.

You don't need to worry about me, Ma. It's like you always told us: a bow knot WILL untie.

I Can't Turn My Mind Off

One of the most infuriating things about being a writer/ creative is when you can't just shut your brain off and enjoy something without deconstructing it, analyzing it, then trying to find a deeper meaning in it. Whether we're talking literature, television or film, I watch something and I'm constantly trying to figure out what makes it work or how it could be improved. When I went to the theater to see the movie Logan (since at the time people were raving about it), this problem of not turning my brain off was with me. Full disclosure, I'm a huge X-Men fan going back to 1979. One of the most pivotal moments of my young life was reading the graphic novel God Loves, Man Kills back in 1982, so this has become the Gold standard for storytelling in comic books since. That being said, I've hated every single X-Men film that's appeared in theaters since 2000. So I went to see Logan carrying all of this mental and emotional fanboy bias, plus high-ass standards for any film — due to a life of being a critic.

I sit there in the movie theater, and while I am genuinely enjoying the film, I am simultaneously breaking down key scenes in my head like John Madden during a football telecast. I'm keeping track of character interactions and whether or not certain reactions fit the canon, while I'm also watching to see how this onscreen interpretation of popular Marvel character Laura/X-23 is going over. I'm sure that the overwhelming majority of the audience is just watching this film without having all of these gears turning inside their heads, but I can't help it. I'm like this with everything. It's both exhausting and exhilarating. When the film is was finally over, I shared some spoiler-free thoughts on Twitter and I scanned my recent texts to see if anyone else saw the movie. However, there were only certain people that I was willing to discuss it with. One prerequisite is that they need to be hypercritical X-Men/comic book/film fans as well. Preferably, fellow writers or creatives. For reasons...

I actually found someone that I could discuss what I had just seen — sans the issue of certain concepts or points of reference flying over their heads during the conversation. As we both hashed out what worked and what didn't, the conversation next brought us to what we wished would've happened or what could've been done better. Mind you, we both thoroughly liked the film. Still we had critiques. Critiques that were even longer than the ones we'd have for films that we absolutely abhorred. This is due to us both being so emotionally invested in the source material for a huge chunk of our lives, plus being writers ourselves. When Prince watched music shows, he'd spend a great deal of time rearranging the music he heard in his own head. Much of the fandom for modern films are the same exact way. In my case? It's especially tough.

Whether I'm reading an article online, watching a film or documentary on Netflix, or checking out an episode of a show, I can't just let it be. Even if it was perfect, my passion would be to break down why it worked. When I used to help people write dialogue for screenplays, one of the examples I used to show how to immediately engage an audience was the opening six minutes of the film The Social Network. Conversely, when I wanted to use an example of a film that did a poor job of utilizing women or writing strong roles for them, past being just objects or minor characters? I used The Social Network as a perfect example. Even though I love that film, I have analyzed it to the point where I am keenly aware of its biggest flaws. Most people would rather leave well enough alone, but I'm a writer and I study this craft inside and out in order to make myself more effective at it. Since I'm essentially work for hire, my livelihood depends on it. Not only that, but being a fan makes it easier for me to pick out the elements to keep if I ever get the opportunity to adapt one of these properties myself.

Quite a few of the rap writers and music journalists I came up reading have now transitioned into roles as creatives in multiple fields. Their new jobs range from being executive producers, consultants, directors, writers and showrunners for television, cable series' and documentaries. Every time I see either someone I used to read or someone I know land a creative position after being a former music journalist, it gives me hope that all the time I've spent watching series and complaining about the episode or season where it jumped the shark (or the part in a film when I could no longer suspend disbelief) might finally be put to good use one day. All of the articles I've written about the various subjects I'm an expert in could result in a position where I can utilize all of this seemingly useless knowledge. The hours I spend in my own head constantly mulling over how to make written pieces better, or what comic book properties, biopics or subjects/events would make for interesting documentaries and films would no longer be for naught.

I'm often writing during the wee hours of the morning. If I'm not constantly re-writing something I've already written while agonizing over whether or not it sucks, I'm researching another piece that, even if I pitched it to numerous sites or outlets, they wouldn't see the value in it — and thus wouldn't pay me to write it anyways. No matter, as I can easily bang out upwards of 3000 words just to post something to Medium, only to see academics cite it for years or other writers reframe it and pitch it to other outlets that will pay them to run it.

I re-wrote this essay a couple more times than I originally anticipated. I wanted to get across just how much shit goes on upstairs and the motivations behind why I do what I do. As a result, you're currently reading the fifth version of this piece. In the first draft, I wasted a full paragraph explaining the role that fandom plays in art/media and the audience's relationship with the creators/writers of the aforementioned art or media. I also got rid of the part where I went into detail about what I thought was wrong with Logan because it detracted from the main point of this piece: I can't ever shut my brain off. See what I mean?

Choices and Legacy:
A Writer's Reflection
On His Station In Life

When I was a kid, I encountered the book The Hitchhiker's Guide To The Galaxy. I read it here and there, but it just never resonated with me like other Sci Fi novels and short stories I'd read at the time. There's a joke in the book where a supercomputer named Deep Thought is asked for the answer to "life, the Universe and everything" in that order. Deep Thought responds that it has an answer but that it will need to think about it for seven and a half million years. Seven and a half million years later, the descendants of those who originally asked the question return to Deep Thought for its answer. He tells them that they're not going to like it before answering with: "Forty-two." Upon hearing the answer, the descendants of the original inquirers voiced their displeasure and Deep Thought counters with, "I checked it very thoroughly and that quite definitely is the answer. I think the problem, to be quite honest with you, is that you've never actually known what the question is."

Douglas Adams's The Hitchhiker's Guide To The Galaxy was first published in North America in 1980; and I was only nine when I first tried to read it. I just didn't get much of the comedy, even though I was already familiar with quick, biting, sardonic humor thanks to watching British comedies on PBS. The action (or utter lack of it) bored me to tears. I didn't really relate to any of the characters or the scenarios presented in it, so I ultimately never delved much into the series. However, as I got older that "Forty-two" sequence stuck out in my head for years before I'd even realized it was a "thing" amongst the Sci Fi/nerd/geek fandom.

As time passed the whole thing only became bigger, and there was a radio show, TV series, and a 2005 feature film adaptation based on the book. I've been thinking about this section a lot lately since I recently turned 42 and I've begun to really ponder my place in life, the Universe and everything my damn self. Many of my peers, contemporaries, and writers I came up reading, are either married, parents, homeowners, or have jobs in academia. Some are editors, screenwriters, and published authors or experts who make regular television appearances and do panel discussions by the time they were 42. Myself, on the other hand? I haven't done many of those things and quite honestly I haven't tried really hard to make them happen. Writers rely on having their work published in multiple publications, and I just don't pitch because every time an outlet turns down a piece I wrote, I take it as a personal offense. Also, I don't really care for doing many of the other things cats in my age range have transitioned to. Problem is, given my advanced age and my unwillingness to play the game, I have to figure out what I'm going to do before I ultimately get squeezed out of this space for good.

I'm not putting forth any real effort towards doing any on-camera work since everyone's currently pivoting to video rather than focusing on long-form content. I haven't tried to really get my podcast going like I should. I haven't pressed the issue to try to get published or secure an adjunct professorship as of yet, and I'm not willing to leave Boston, which automatically eliminates any possible job opportunities in New York City or Los Angeles.

If I'm open to being a music supervisor in film and television or consulting on a documentary or a TV show or film, then I should really do things that put me in position to be chosen for one of those jobs. Or I should get off my ass and get my own project off the ground, seeing as this space cares less and less about all the things I happen to specialize in. The writing's been on the wall

107

for years, but I keep getting stays of execution. Sooner or later my luck will finally run out.

I recently had an idea for a string of pieces I had proposed for the Summer (which is now over) that I referred to as "legacy content". My heart sank at reading this characterization of what I feel were necessary pieces honoring the importance of crucial and influential albums to the rap music continuum. It hit me that I don't see what I do as "content." I never have.

In my mind, I'm doing a service by putting something into its proper historical context. Everything I write is personal, not business — even though I get paid to do so. I've deleted this very piece I'm writing four times already because I wasn't feeling it. I agonize over every sentence I type. I need to feel an emotional connection to the subject matter of each of article write. That's a problem.

At the end of the day, I'm work-for-hire and this is a job. Writers don't often have the luxury of only writing about what they want and not being slaves to deadlines. Shit, I'm gonna write about what I want to regardless. I wrote 2500 words about the lasting influence of the summer of 1987 knowing damn well no one else would want to run it, and I could write similar pieces every week. This is the worst time imaginable to be a 42-year-old expert in multiple fields and stuck in your ways. It feels really No Country For Old Men in this field presently.

Turning 42 made me realize that I'm now closer to death than anything else. I've seen many of my peers and contemporaries die in their 40s in recent years, which makes me think about my legacy and hyper-conscious about my voice and impact. I constantly think about how I'll be remembered or what holes or voids of information I've already filled in the past versus what's still left to cover. If I haven't written a long-form piece about it, I've probably broken it down on Instagram or Twitter because fewer people seem willing to read, and it's a pain in the ass to find someone willing to pay you to write about it if they can't ensure it'll bring in a certain amount of site visits and page views. I'm so in my head when I write articles that I don't even think about site traffic or numbers, merely about whether I'm expressing myself as honestly as humanly possible in a way that might resonate with readers.

At this point, I've decided that the most important thing for me as a writer is not to be a careerist and concern myself with upward mobility even though at this stage in my life I should be far more successful than I currently am. Fact of the matter is, I prefer to have the freedom to do whatever I want and write about whatever I feel like as opposed to feeling obligated to cover a subject I don't care about because it's "hot" at the moment. I can't succumb to societal pressures and gauge what I'm doing at this age on what others did at my age because we are not the same and do not possess the same motivations or impetus. If I had a wife, kids, or a mortgage, I more than likely would've played the game and I'd have a high-profile job by now. Since I don't, I can continue to define my success on my own terms and on whatever timetable I find acceptable.

I have to be proud of myself and my output first and foremost. As long as I can personally stand behind every single article or piece I've written without feeling like I comprised my integrity or sold my soul in the process. I've figured out the answer to everything — and the question — at 42. I totally understand my role and place in the Universe and I truly feel like what I do is my life's calling. I guess Deep Thought was right after all.

Part 4
FRESH PERSPECTIVES

Fans of the Internet Age: From Bravado to Emotion and The Evolution of Rap Content from Mystique and Mystery to Everything Laid Bare

In recent years, I've noticed that the aesthetic of what an emcee is supposed to be like and sound like has changed drastically from what it's been in the past. So much so that emcees and rappers from bygone eras who are still in the game look at the rappers of today (late 2010s) in disgust and sometimes even disbelief. Even older fans aren't immune. They just don't understand what the new breed of emcee's allure is.

When the late Brooklyn rap legend Sean Price appeared on the Combat Jack Show (ca. 2012), he was asked what was the meaning behind his now infamous line, "I don't Wale them new niggas." Sean plainly answered that it wasn't even a diss, but merely a truthful statement: "These new rappers? I just don't do what they do". He Price also went on to explain why he avoided Twitter, saying that Rakim wouldn't have been on Twitter back in the days "talkin' about, "I'm studying 120 right now."

Think about the popular rappers right now like Drake, Kendrick Lamar, Kanye West, Kid Cudi, Travis Scott, etc. Now think about some other rappers with devoted underground followings like Joe Budden and Jay Electronica. What do they all have in common? They pretty much put it all out there for their fans and make emotionally charged, personal music. When I was coming up, rappers, for the most part, portrayed themselves as superheroes. They were all-powerful masters of ceremony. Think back to how fans perceived the Cold Crush Brothers, Fantastic 5, Funky Four Plus One, Crash Crew, Grandmaster Flash & The Furious Five, Treacherous Three, Fearless 4 on down to Run DMC, LL Cool J, Kurtis Blow and the like. When I first saw Wild Style, I thought that it was the greatest thing ever recorded on film in my opinion. These gods were recorded doing their things on celluloid so we mere mortals could finally see what they looked like. Can you grasp that concept? We barely had album covers back in 1982 & and 1983, so just seeing Grandmaster Caz and Grandmaster Flash in action blew my mind.

When I saw Run get slapped in the face by Sheila E in the movie Krush Groove, I was completely in shock. It was as if someone kicked the Pope in the balls. I couldn't even fathom something like that ever happening to DJ Run. He wasn't a regular human to us. He was in Run DMC. The Kings From Queens! This was partly due to the fact that we had limited media access to these artists in the early/mid-'80s. And it was this limited access that helped them attain a larger-than-life image. Doug E. Fresh had been making records for years by then and had even been in movies, but I didn't see a good quality picture of Doug E. Fresh until I saw a flier with his face on it back in 1985 for God's sake.

At that time, urban music magazines like Right On! and Black Beat were not equipped to cover hip hop music or the culture seriously; and mainstream publications only mentioned hip hop in passing. If you didn't have access to The Village Voice or similar NYC publications, then most of your hip hop news was third or fourth-hand at best. It wasn't until magazines like The Source and Rap Pages began publishing that we even got an idea of what was up with our hip hop icons and rap idols.

Slick Rick was large. He had the furs, eyepatch, mad dookie ropes and the rings. Big Daddy Kane always had the fresh outfits. Eric B. & Rakim were no joke. Ultramagnetic MC's were from another universe entirely. Stetsasonic was the ultimate hip hop band, complete with matching outfits. Public Enemy were the prophets of rage. They all were revered like Blaxploitation film heroes; each deserved their own Marvel comics title. They were untouchable. They were our heroes. We don't remember them being anything less than the images they portrayed. If you grew up with this aesthetic for what an emcee or rapper is supposed to be, then you'll find an emcee like Drake to be a disappointment. He gets too personal and offers far too much about his own life. He raps about how he's disappointing his mother and how he feels trapped by fame. Oldheads feel the urge to scream, "Man the fuck up!" at their own iPods during a Drake song.

Even a skilled rapper like Joe Budden, who makes what he calls "mood music", gets extremely personal in his music. He discusses his past addiction, his relationship with his family and his son, and his failed relationships, even his current ones online. Before he had his own hit podcast, he even recorded his life and on UStreams. often for his fans. Oldheads could do without all the access even though it makes his fans anticipate "Mood Music 4" even more. Leave something to the imagination, dammit!

But the bottom line is that the paradigm has shifted, due largely to media accessibility and changes in technology over the past 13 years. So the new breed of fans have actually become emotionally invested in these artists in ways that we never were. Fans today feel as if they're watching the underdog come up. This is the same dynamic that made fans connect to the Notorious B.I.G. and Jay-Z in the '90s. Listen to Ready To Die (1994) and Reasonable Doubt (1996) by B.I.G. and Jay-Z respectively and tell me that you don't come away without feeling emotionally invested in either cat of those artists. It's impossible not to do so.

In the '90s, fans thought that they were watching the ascension of the former hustler make his way (legitimately) in the music industry. Their back stories made you root for them. This also worked with Tupac Shakur. The thing is that you had to work to get details about these artists' real lives. They were each compelling subjects for hip hop journalists. Even when they went through things and shared their low points with the public, through their music or the media, they never seemed completely vulnerable. They always dealt from a position of power. To this day, there are a great amount of things about or favorite older emcee's lives and careers we know nothing about. We can't necessarily say that about this generation of artists because everything is often out in the open and laid bare.

Back in the days, when an artist had issues with their group members or labels, you found out about it later. There was a delay in news; and even then you weren't privy to their exact words and/ or actions during the dispute. Nowadays, with the internet and the hundreds of blogs, video sites, Twitter, and Facebook you can see it all unfold in real time. There's no more mystery. No more mystique.

Being that I (and most fans from my same generation) grew up seeing rappers as superheroes and mysterious beings beyond our understanding, there's no mystery why the subsequent generations of rappers would become increasingly more and more human as time passed. The problem is that the lines between artists and the people consuming their music have been blurred.

Take a rapper like Charles Hamilton. He was so open about his life and shared so much in his music and online via his blog that he attained a cult-like following of fans in a short time. He often made himself so vulnerable to the public that it was unnerving. Old-head fans hated his whole persona with a passion. He dropped a full mixtape of free music every month and he was always around. The old adage "Absence makes the heart grow fonder" meant nothing to him. Ultimately, overexposure — and him making one too many mistakes in the public eye —led to him losing his deal with Interscope, and he became a pariah.

Traditional gender roles have also shifted in recent years, what some refer to as the "pussification of the modern man," resulting in men who wear tight clothing, are immaculately groomed, and willingly discuss their feelings without prodding. Those of us who grew up playing on playgrounds made of concrete rather than soft foam aren't feeling this new breed of rapper at all. We want less Travie McCoy and more Ghostface Killah. Butch it up, homie! The hipster aspect is completely lost on older rap fans who also don't understand the allure of many of the so called popular "blog rappers".

In the late '90s and early '00s, DMX would often cry on stage while doing his prayers. But few people clowned him for it. This is because fans felt emotionally invested in him. Even when he was in a vulnerable state, DMX was still highly regarded in the hip hop world the same as Busta Rhymes, Jay-Z, Redman, Raekwon, and Scarface to name a few fellow icons — each earning emotional investment without much or anything at all being known about their backstory. But as I've said, things have changed, and in the past decade, many rappers have earned emotional investment from fans largely because of their backstories. In this regard, rappers like Eminem, Beanie Sigel, T.I., Joe Budden, Kanye West, 50 Cent, Young Jeezy, Maino, Drake, and Kendrick Lamar come to mind. The back stories of these rappers range from having adverse childhoods, to being former drug dealers and to recently getting out of jail to surviving shootings or car accidents and much more. In each case, music fans bought into their backstories and their music.

When these artists got personal, whether it was in their music or in magazine articles, fans ate it up. Jay-Z had been around since 1988, but fans were still looking forward to his book Decoded because there was still so much about his life that we didn't know, despite the fact that he'd been hot for more than two decades. Now that accessible media publishing tools like Ustream,

YouTube, Blogger, Wordpress and Tumblr have helped to blurred the lines between artist and fans, there is seems to be less need for investigative reporting about our "mysterious" new young artists because they talk directly to the fans from jump.

But mystery can still work. Look at Lady Gaga. That chick is so weird that even though we know her full government name, who her parents and siblings are, as well as the timeline and full story of how she broke into the music industry, she's still an enigma. Gaga holds back, but she gives just enough to the fans of the Internet Age that she can entertain them and still actually sell records. She may be the era's exception, though.

My boy ST/MiC is a producer, audio engineer, and an emcee. He specializes in remixes and is a Bruce Lee fan (as am I). He has always been attracted to beats or production and songs with what he terms "emotional content". For him it's all about if that beat, those bars, or that song can elicit an emotional reaction from him. If it can, he'll buy it. Furthermore, Bruce Lee always stressed that it was more important to fight with emotion (or rather emotional content) than anger because the only thing that anger does is cloud your judgement. By infusing emotional content into your attacks, it suggested that you were the one in control. I'm the same way as my boy ST/MiC and Bruce Lee. And for me, it's also about what kind of music elicits an emotional reaction in me versus what would instead repulse me.

For instance, let's take Kanye West's 808s & Heartbreak and Kid Cudi's Man In The Moon. I reviewed Kanye West's deeply personal, Electro-tinged and AutoTune-heavy 808s & Heartbreak a while back. While I gave it a positive review, I felt that I was hearing music of a nature so personal that I almost shouldn't be listening to it. Not only that, but the aesthetic of the beats and music on this album just weren't my thing.

On the other side, Kid Cudi's Man In The Moon fared slightly better with me. The album still felt too emo and personal for my tastes, but in order to give a fair listen I decided to regard it like a pop/soul LP in the vein of Kenna rather than a rap/hip hop album. And in that case, it was a damn good album. I also haven't played 808s or Man In The Moon since I reviewed them, opting instead to play albums in the vein of Roc Marciano's Marcberg or Danny Brown's The Hybrid. Much like most older rap fans, I'm just not a fan of giving everything about yourself away. Especially things that might make you look like a sucker. The kind of shit we just didn't do or tolerate back in the days just seems to be regular practice now.

Since the distance between the fan and the artist has gotten closer as the years pass and artists become more and more human, it's tough to make the average cynic fan a believer. In this current world, everything seems to get a pass. Rick Ross was revealed to be a complete liar. Lupe Fiasco had regular bitch fits when his songs leaked to blogs and when his record label didn't do what he wanted them to do. And "blog rappers" get beat up and/or robbed on camera, and it ends up on World Star Hip Hop the next day. The only challenge that remains is whether or not if you can move the crowd. Not necessarily physically, but emotionally. But the age of boom bap rap on the mainstream is dead. So it seems like the only thing left to do is it's time to tighten up your pants, rock some shiny ass Supras, cop a smedium hoody with glitter on it and get emo. And if you can carry a tune then you better sing your hooks. Look at how the branding Diggy Simmons was initially branded at Atlantic now Records, for God's sake!

Older hip hop fans just lament the old hip hop aesthetic of being larger than life or invincible. LL Cool J gave off the same air and he made songs like "I Want You", "I Need Love", "One Shot At Love" and "Two Different Worlds". And even when LL got dissed relentlessly by the hip hop world at large, as a result, was depressed about it, his sulking and moping was done in private. Later on, he appeared on the scene with a new hot song and he was that same monster again. Today, however, artists will record a video of themselves — showcasing their own vulnerable times and personal breakdowns — then upload it for the entire world to see. In a time where younger fans have grown up with reality TV, these events can be spun into buzz or something positive. Meanwhile, all it does is turn the stomachs of older rap fans that grew up in an era where shit like that would've gotten you clowned out of the game entirely. We are currently entrenched in an era of emo rap where rappers simply share too much of themselves, and there seems to be no end in sight.

Things won't ever go back to the way they used to be so forget about it. We are dealing with a new breed of fans today, and largely because of this we are also dealing with a new breed of artists. Fans interact with artists and vice versa in real time now. Not to mention, we're dealing with different industry dynamics. Media oversaturation and technological advancements have removed most of the mystery and distance artists and fans enjoyed in the past. Furthermore, gossip and celebrity news — both on television and the internet in tandem with the wide proliferation of reality television — has shaped how the post-Telecommunications Act fan views their favorite artists, as well as what they expect from them in terms of image. Fans of the internet age will simply let more slide because it's not a leap for them like it is for fans from decades ago.

An 18 - 25 year old hip hop fan today was born between 1985 and 1992. The Telecommunications Act passed in 1996 (it took until 1997 for the byproducts to begin to take effect) and there is a new generation of urban music every three to five years. Stay with me on this. The average ages that someone first develops their taste in music or becomes aware of it personally are the ages of 9 and 13. If you were born in 1985 that would land you between 1994 and 1998, fully entrenched in the post-Telecommunications Act era of music, radio and television networks as well as the reality television era. To fans in this age range, the change hasn't been as drastic to start and seems pretty organic. It's the same for their younger siblings who are also part of the same demographic. But to us fans that remember what it was like before, the world has turned upside down.

Where's Hip Hop's *High Fidelity* and *Almost Famous*? (And Why *Brown Sugar* Ain't It)

Two of my all-time favorite films are *High Fidelity* (2000) and *Almost Famous* (2000).. High Fidelity is a semi-autobiographical film about a young rock writer based on Cameron Crowe's time spent as a teenaged rock journalist during the early '70s. One Almost Famous is an adaptation of Nick Hornby's novel of the same name about a thirty-something, music-obsessed record store owner dealing with his most recent break up. Both films are everything a music and film-loving, former record store worker would love. And both films present a few things that should stand to Gen X'ers like myself.

First both films were released in 2000, during an interesting span of six months (between March 31st and September 15th). The Dot Com Bubble had just recently burst; several companies saw their stock shares plummet and the entire tech sector was in complete upheaval. Anyone that was either employed by a startup or was operating one was really going through it during this time. At this same time, we were deeply entrenched in the Napster Era. Broad access to P2P sites like Napster and LimeWire caused large-scale traditional brick and mortar music stores to see a significant drop in sales.

Even independent record stores were beginning to feel the squeeze. I should know, I worked at a used CD/DVD store (RIP CD Spins) at the time, and before that I had been a manager at Tower Records. When I first saw High Fidelity, it was like seeing my life (parts of it, at least) playing out in front of me.

High Fidelity represented a time before independent record stores began disappearing left and right, a time when I had multiple vinyl spots to frequent. There was no internet 24/7 back then, so the record store itself served as our social network. This era is forever preserved in amber with *High Fidelity*.

I was still working at CD Spins (though I quit that same month) when I first saw Almost Famous. While I was there, I read a lot of books — two that still stand out to me now are Legs McNeil's Please Kill Me and a beat up, dog eared paperback copy of Psychotic Reactions and Carburetor Dung by Lester Bangs that we kept behind the counter at all times. We'd often have rock debates on and off in the store (and directly outside of it) that customers would join in on. Almost Famous was one of those films that spoke to those of us that fell in love with music at a young age and never let go of it, much like William Miller, the protagonist in the film.

As I think about *High Fidelity* and *Almost Famous*, I can't help but notice that hip hop does not have any films equivalent to either of them. Considering that hip hop culture is 40 years old, rap music has appeared in recorded form for more than 35 years, and May 4th, 2014 marked the 30th anniversary of Breakin,' the first major studio hip hop film. And NO, Brown Sugar doesn't count. When you watch Brown Sugar, at no point do you get the feeling that the main characters really ate, lived, and breathed hip hop. I mean, they say that they do, but there's no real conviction in those onscreen performances. Compare the (short) scene where Sidney and Dre are discussing hip hop to the dinner scene in Almost Famous where the wide eyed William Miller speaks to Lester Bangs (played masterfully by the late Philip Seymour Hoffman). The sequence in Brown Sugar almost seems forced, like there were certain details or specific songs that the actors were told to mention between takes. I've had hip hop discussions with people that love hip hop as much as I do. Long ones and short ones. And let me tell you, that shit in Brown Sugar was neither authentic nor believable. It's the writer's job to make the audience suspend disbelief. Towards that end, this scene in Brown Sugar fails miserably.

To this point, in Ava DuVernay's brilliant film I Will Follow Maye, the main character, has a discussion with her nephew Raven about Nas. and That scene is great. It's totally believable, no one who actually loves hip hop couldn't suspend disbelief because it looked and sounded like a real rap debate/discussion between two heads. Mind you, I Will Follow is about various themes far removed from music, but that small scene alone rendered Brown Sugar moot and unwatchable.

If you contrast the soulless scenes in which Sidney and Dre discuss hip hop in Brown Sugar, in which they only discuss hip hop in passing and never go into any type of real detail, with the the passionate music discussions Rob has with his employees Dick and Barry at Championship Vinyl in High Fidelity, you can further understand my point. I could relate to those scenarios immediately because I lived it. However, I don't recall ever having such a subdued conversation about hip hop as Sidney and Dre had while reminiscing about the things I truly love above hip hop.

There was no point in Almost Famous where I didn't believe that William Miller didn't love rock with every fiber of his being. I completely bought that Penny Lane and her Band Aids were so enamored with the music that they willingly gave of themselves to become muses (amongst other things) for rock stars. In their roles as Russell Hammond and Jeff Bebe of Stillwater, I believed every single word that Billy Crudup and Jason Lee uttered on film (I think the "Tiny Dancer" sing along cemented a lot). Now as a 40-something hip hop fan, where's my version of this kind of experience captured on film? Where's my hip hop equivalent of a music nerd moment in a dramatic film?

Many hip hop heads (especially those who are journalists like myself) swear by both High Fidelity and Almost Famous. Donwill, of the Rap group Tanya Morgan, even made an amazing 2011 concept album called Don Cusack in High Fidelity, an album entirely inspired by the film High Fidelity. His video for "Laura's Song" was shot in Fat Beats (RIP) and replicated notable scenes from the film.

Hip hop heads related to this film High Fidelity because we saw music fans that were passionate just like we were. But we just don't see anything made for hip hop that depicts it the same manner Hollywood films depicts rock. Is it too much to ask to see a major studio film that gives hip hop the respect, genuine love, or and gravity that the culture and art form truly deserves? As we all know, it ultimately comes down to numbers. Let's not be naive here. Even when rap overtook country as the #1 selling music genre between 1997 and 2000, film studios were still hesitant at to releasing release hip hop-related films outside of documentaries. Of the hip hop-related dramas that were released during this period — Belly, Slam, Ghost Dog, Black & White, etc. — none of them had the backers, producers, writers, directors, budget or cache equivalent to what High Fidelity or Almost Famous had.

High Fidelity was an adaptation of a best-selling novel that was highly anticipated, and Almost Famous had Cameron Crowe at the helm as a writer/director. Classic rock (repackaged over and over) has been the music industry's chief money maker since the inception of the LP as the new industry standard (as opposed to the double sided 7" 45 RPM single), so they had a built-in audience and nostalgia on their side from the outset. In short, rock is the industry wide "default setting" and we'd be hard pressed to find multiple people who grew up in hip hop culture in positions of power at major film studios.

Earlier, I mentioned Ava DuVernay's scene from I Will Follow that actually captured the aesthetic of an authentic discussion between two hip hop fans. The reason that that scene is authentic is because it was written by an actual hip hop fan. Ava DuVernay was part of the burgeoning LA underground hip hop scene during the early '90s, and in 2008 she made a brilliant documentary about the legendary Good Life Café, which later gave birth to Project Blowed (think the Nuyorican Poets Cafe meets The Lyricist Lounge in NYC, but it was first) titled This Is The Life.

Last year writer/director Neil Drumming released the hip hop themed drama Big Words, a film about an influential underground rap group fifteen years removed from their glory days. The dialogue and personal interaction between the characters in Big Words rang as true because they were written by an actual hip hop fan in his late '30s who grew up in and around the culture between 1979 and the present day.

Although Michael Elliott, the writer of Brown Sugar, grew up with hip hop and was a former writer for The Source magazine, he had no real say in the film's direction, as he didn't produce (Peter Heller, Trish Hofmann and Magic Johnson did) or direct it (Rick Famuyiwa did). I can guarantee you that neither Peter Heller nor Trish Hofmann were overly concerned about whether or not the exchanges about hip hop would come across as authentic to the true heads watching this film. That wasn't a priority. The only concerns were, just is there enough comedy in it and is it marketable enough to cross over to a mainstream audience? These obviously weren't the concerns when making either High Fidelity or Almost Famous.

In Almost Famous, there are multiple scenes where William's big sister Anita argues with her mother about the artistic value of rock music. I remember having similar debates with my own mother, defending rap by contrasting her feelings about rap to her own stories about how the elders reacted when rock and R&B became popular with the young people during her teenage years in the deep South. When Anita finally leaves home after another row with her mother, and gives William her hidden album collection, I was emotionally invested in the film from that moment on. Cameron Crowe knew exactly how that sequence would affect viewers and get them all to buy into what were undoubtedly the beginning stages of Wiliam's love affair and intense passion for rock. Question is, who's going to do the same or something similar for hip hop in film?

The answer to my previous question stares back at me every time I look in a mirror. The truth is that no one is going to make these film except for those of us who actually wonder where they are. No one will care to make a film centered around our experiences growing up with hip hop culture and the music that gives it the treatment, love and respect it deserves. No major film studio will make it a priority to create films that value authenticity over marketability and crossover potential to accurately show the sheer beauty, depth and complexity contained with the culture of hip hop culture. This is why I say that It's time that we become our own Cameron Crowes, create our own Dreamworks SKG, write, produce, direct, market, promote and support the type of films that the Hollywood system refuses to make. There are organizations like AFFRM, Film Independent, The Sundance Institute (Film Forward & Women Filmmakers Initiative), IFC Films, etc., in addition to crowd funding options like Kickstarter and Indiegogo, to help filmmakers and producers tell their stories and get them distributed. It all starts with us. If enough of these kinds of films are made that resonate with audiences and make them take notice then, and ONLY then, will anyone inside the Hollywood system even consider doing the same.

In closing, what we tend to forget — or what many still do not know — is that Breakin', the first major studio hip hop culture-related film, was preceded by the films Style Wars and Wild Style in 1983. In 1984, after Hollywood realized that there was interest in hip hop culture and a potential payday, they plundered these two independent films for characters and storylines for their own studio films: Breakin', Beat Street, Body Rock, and Breakin' 2: Electric Boogaloo. For Hollywood, it was about capitalizing on a rising fad and making a quick buck rather than showcasing the brilliance of this new American culture and art form that would soon become a global culture. Authenticity be damned.

We won't see the type of films that take hip hop culture seriously enough to treat it with the same respect and care they do with rock until a precedent is set that forces them to do so. In the meantime, I'll continue to watch High Fidelity and Almost Famous and hope that that this piece helps bring about the creation of the exact kind of films I want to see one day. Who knows, maybe the kind of films I'll make one day.

An Alternate Take On The Perception Of Nas' *Illmatic* 20 Years Later

Illmatic, Nas's debut album, is regarded as an unadulterated rap classic and is arguably the greatest hip hop album ever recorded. When Nas first came on the scene, he was considered the second coming of Rakim, and his album Illmatic was declared a classic months before it ever even surfaced. The Queens rapper's album was highly anticipated and it received a perfect rating from The Source, with the review being written by a young Minya Oh AKA Miss Info as Shortie. Even with all of the critical acclaim that the album earned at the time, it failed to sell well due to a combination of heavy bootlegging and the lack of a hit single on the radio or in the clubs.

To further put things into perspective, the day that Illmatic dropped Shyheim's debut album, AKA The Rugged Child, was also released and it outsold Illmatic off the strength of his hit single "On & On." While Nas had all the critical acclaim one could wish for, a dream team of producers, and The Source magazine (the Bible of hip hop itself) cheerleading for him, the best he could muster was selling 59,000 units in his opening week. I know you're wondering what this has to do with the album being an unadulterated masterpiece both lyrically and in term of production? I'm getting to that.

At the time Illmatic was released, rap fans focused on the quality of the album rather than its sales numbers. The only reason I even know how many units Illmatic moved its opening week is because MC Serch, executive producer of Illmatic, revealed the numbers in a appearance on Cipha Sounds and Peter Rosenberg's Juan Epstein podcast. I wasn't aware that none of Illmatic's singles were hits (although "It Ain't Hard To Tell" actually succeeded at cracking the Billboard Hot 100, it peaked at #91) until I checked the Billboard charts numbers recently. But sales numbers aren't things that even the most knowledgeable hip hop head cared about in 1994.

However, in 2018, everything is about sales, numbers, chart position, spins, "hotness" and "relevance." It's odd to see those who don't appreciate the more lyrical, creative, and artistic rap of the day (let's be honest, they just ignore it) heap praise on Illmatic, considering if it came out today they'd probably think it was boring.

"Nas' debut album was purposely built to stand the test of time and age like Pharrell Williams."

If Illmatic dropped today, many of the bloggers who talk about what a masterpiece it was would clown it's opening week sales and its it sounds "dated" sound. They'd remark that Nas needs production from DJ Mustard or Mike Will Made It and guest verses from 2 Chainz or Nicki Minaj. They'd treat him exactly like they do Roc Marciano and Ka today, like he's a second or third-tier citizens, when in reality they make some of the most concise, timeless hip hop albums of the present day rap world.

Illmatic was not an easily accessible rap project by any stretch of the imagination. It was geared towards those who appreciated music from previous eras and challenged the listener. It was dense, and layered, and took multiple listens to grasp even though it was short by 1994 rap album standards. In many ways, it was a jazz album made for those who had the attention spans and a high enough level of maturity to fully accept it. It forced multiple producers to all get on the same page to craft a concise rap album, with no notable guest appearances other than then-unsigned rapper AZ, who was featured on "Life's A Bitch," the song that Nas received The Source's Hip-Hop Quotable Rhyme Of The Month.

In an era of short attention spans and radio or club pandering, Illmatic sounds out of place; reason being is because it's an example of painstakingly crafted art in an era of disposable music. It kills me that I see people who praise this album yet ignore modern rap made that follow its example. Everything about Illmatic was made to appeal to a specialized audience as opposed to chasing big sales numbers. Illmatic was purposely built to stand the test of time and age like Pharrell Williams. Each song was made with the mindset that it was part of a greater body of work. The album opens with "The Genesis," which uses music from the score of the film Wild Style as well as audio from the film's opening scene. In 1994, few people outside of New York had even seen Wild Style to fully grasp the significance of the album's intro. Wild Style wasn't widely available for sale or rental on VHS at the time, and the only places to purchase it were mail order ads in the back of The Source or from catalogs in imported graffiti magazines. Illmatic was not easily accessible music that catered to the listener, you had to take three steps towards it. Nas is the son of a Jazz musician and bluesman, after all.

The reason so many heads of my generation fell in love with Illmatic is because it dredged up nostalgic feelings when music meant so much more to our lives, when we all huddled around the radio because it reflected the voice of our community and was genuinely invested in our well being. Back then, records seemed to perfectly capture the spirit and flavor of the times they were made in. Illmatic drew directly from the classic albums of the past and, in turn, it inspired many classic albums of the future.

Illmatic is praised today and regarded as a classic even though it was overshadowed by The Notorious B.I.G.'s classic debut, Ready To Die, which was powered by the hit singles "Juicy" and "One More Chance." Nas and Illmatic also failed to receive any accolades at the 1995 Source Awards from — the same magazine that in the previous year had regarded him as the "Second Coming of Rakim." In 2014, which marked the 20th anniversary of Illmatic, there were multiple think pieces, retrospectives, mini documentaries, and the Tribeca Film Festival premiere of Time Is Illmatic. Amazing considering it took this same album more than two years to initially go gold and another five years after that to go platinum. I can't wait to see what they do for Ready To Die's 20th anniversary!

Jay-Z Is A Business, Man: The New Rules for the Few In The New Age of Rap Marketing

This is the "event" era of rap releases apparently. You can't just make a quality album, promote it, and hope that it resonates with people and builds momentum through word of mouth anymore. Now, It's about generating massive amounts of buzz through hype — via social networks and blogs — until people on the streets are talking about said synthesized event. It happened with Watch The Throne (Jay-Z & Kanye West). It happened again with Yeezus (Kanye West. Now let's explore the repercussions, byproducts and reactions to how the project was marketed, shall we?

Take for example Jay'z album Magna Carta Holy Grail. The whole marketing plan behind Magna Carta Holy Grail kicked off in grand fashion. It's premier commercial aired during a key NBA Finals game (in a hotly contested series) and was sponsored by Samsung. Jay-Z is no brand loyalist by any stretch of the imagination, mind you. In the past he's released sneakers with Reebok while he wore Adidas regularly, and he's done commercials with HP while he was photographed using Apple laptops. The company/brand that put up the money was irrelevant, all that really mattered was Jay-Z got them to pay him and fund his next endeavor. Something that no other rapper in the game at that time was is in the position to do.

Jay-Z was lavished with praise for being a savvy businessman who went platinum three weeks before his new album even came out. He'd taken the steam out of a June 18th release date, a date on which the entire industry also decided to release an album The Magna Carta Holy Grail app wouldn't become downloadable until

June 24th. No one had bought a Samsung phone yet. No one had even heard a full song from the album yet, but people were already making declarations. Wait. WHAT?

There was talk about how Samsung had won already. First off, how long would it be before any sales numbers were reported on Samsung phones and tablets before that could be confirmed? Secondly, common sense would dictate that we wait to see how the app itself actually functions before declaring it a success. In addition, we'd have to contrast how Apple iPhones and iPads sold during the same period without have any entertainers use their brand to sell their new or previous existing products to consumers. That's what we call "data". Without it, it's tough to arrive at a conclusion. Since none of us are Loopers let's just wait and see what happens first, OK?

Around this dame time, Jay-Z had turned Havana into Atlanta, and the film adaptation of one of the Great American Novels The Great Gatsby into "Idlewild". We'd entered a stretch where movies either had a Jay-Z or a Kanye West song in their trailers. It has been made clear that Jay-Z and Kanye West were by far the most palatable rappers to corporations. Kanye West had decided to spurn the advances of corporations, partnerships, and sponsorships this time around. Instead, he wanted to rub shoulders with creatives and artists in varying fields in Paris. This left Jay-Z alone in the wilderness with an AK-47 and night vision goggles while everyone else had torches, spears and arrows.

Jay-Z spoke of and tweeted about "New Rules" in this new digital age the day after his commercial aired. This is true, because in this new world, where the business model is constantly changing and we have infinite choice, the playing field is leveled somewhat because a "nobody" can elevate themselves due to the internet's democratization of everything. But Jay-Z then said something completely counter to his point right afterwards. He wanted to gather everyone around the radio like they did in the old days for his next event. The radio? When people gathered around the radio for a big event, there was little to no choice. What Jay-Z's "New Rules" were talking about was essentially finding a way to monopolize people's time and draw everyone's eyes to him at a time where everyone's attention was split.

Jay-Z tweeted about the #NewRules and how Kanye West had the 66 building projection sites for "New Slaves" and "Yeezus" had no lead single or video, and how J.Cole had the digital listening sessions for his new album Born Sinner (in some of the most tech-savvy cities in America, so his album leaked immediately afterwards). These were definitely innovative promotional attempts, but their impact was too new to establish them as being a part of any "new rules". Instead, they were new forms of marketing in a changing digital landscape. These new forms marketing couldn't even be considered successful yet. That didn't stop people from taking Jay-Z's tweets and running with them as if they were gospel.

Jay-Z tweeted about Billboard not recognizing the million albums given away for free as being sold copies. The RIAA then decided to change their rules and have them count, which bypasses both Billboard and Soundscan. Let's recap. Jay-Z made a partnership with a communications company where they sell and market his album and help boost their brand. In addition, it's already platinum before the album is even downloaded by consumers or even available for purchase. I don't know about you, but that sounds like sales fixing rather than brilliant business to me. The reach was already guaranteed, the buzz was guaranteed, the sales were even guaranteed. Where was the innovation again?

Let's talk about the Magna Carta Holy Grail app itself for a moment. Shortly after it became available,there were problems with it. In the end, however, the technical issues with the app were of no real consequence. If the app worked better with Apple product users than Samsung users wasn't even an issue (although I think that is was a serious issue as an Apple loyalist). Jay-Z made out like a bandit even though his album leaked. He got his buzz, money, and sales for his new album. But Samsung ultimately dropped the ball and failed to deliver basic things in epic fashion. Now about those "New Rules"...

In order for any of these supposed New Rules Jay-Z is talking about to be valid, they have to be able to be implemented by more than only five people on the face of the Earth. Who else besides Jay-Z would be able to convince a conglomerate like Samsung to partner with him in order to release his album and promote it via an app they'd develop and make available on their phones and tablets? How many artists could even possibly sway people to buy a new handheld device simply because they were associated with it? Now ask yourself what rappers could do any of this? Certainly not enough for these so-called New Rules to matter since they apply to almost no one else.

Between Yeezus and Magna Carta Holy Grail, there's been a central theme of high art, opulence, and wealth, things that are just not accessible to the majority of the populace. People in the rap industry constantly praise Jay-Z's business savvy and cite him as an example to follow. Just one thing, though: You CAN'T follow him. You can't do what he does. His coups and successes aren't ones you can readily emulate. At least not anymore, you can't.

Former drug dealer Notorious B.I.G. gained mainstream acceptance and subsequently made it possible for Jay-Z to do the same. Jay-Z's crossover success and corporate attractiveness made it possible for 50 Cent to follow in his footsteps and also enter the corporate arena. Post 2010, Jay-Z's reach and influence have grown to near unattainable levels by any rapper who's career began after 2000. Much like the theory of Trickle Down Economics, his windfalls won't positively affect us in the rest of the rap game. From now on, every time Jay-Z raises the bar he's just putting it further out of reach for everyone else.

And I must say that Magna Carta Holy Grail is not a bad album. It's certainly better than that clusterfuck of an album The Blueprint 3 or even Watch The Throne, the event album that put us on this current trajectory. It's far more accessible than Yeezus. The problem is that Jay often sounds like other people other than Jay-Z when he raps on MCHG. In some spots he sounds like someone's 43 year old uncle on the mic rapping over beats that are too young for him using other cats' flows. This is something Jay-Z should never do. No matter. He did numbers, as he'll always do his numbers regardless. He gets paid no matter what. No harm, no foul. Jay-Z's not a businessman. HE'S A BUSINESS, MAN!

Jay-Z is at a stage in his career that no other rapper has entered before. He remained a huge commercial draw and relevant in the music industry after 13 solo albums and 22 years. He's 48 years old in a game where 30 is considered old. When I was a kid, most rappers were between the ages of 16 and 20, and the idea of 30 year olds rapping one day never even dawned on us back then. Everything from here on for Jay-Z is previously undiscovered territory. He once elaborated on Young Chris' flow a decade ago, and before that he used inspiration from Nas, Biggie, and Big L to craft Reasonable Doubt. However, back then it wasn't as obvious as it is now.

Business trumping art isn't anything new in this modern era of rap. The issue is that we're entering into a dangerous new era where the album and music itself is secondary to the synthesis of the event. The business deal and marketing of a project is a bigger story than the album is. No one was even willing to wait to see what happened with the full album roll out of Magna Carta Holy Grail before speculating on what Jay's new Samsung deal meant for the music industry first. The June 29, 2013 issue of Billboard magazine hit newsstands five days before the album was even available for download and more than a week before it went on sale. The story itself was bigger than the album. The music is secondary to the commerce behind it. No one even knew what the album sounded like when it went to press. It simply didn't matter.

While I wouldn't compare the Magna Carta Holy Grail and Yeezus to each other, I have no issue comparing the events surrounding them. Kanye West opted to forgo releasing a commercial single, video, or even allow for any pre-orders of his album. Kanye West didn't want to partner with any corporations or conglomerates this time around. When it came time to let people hear it, he opted against forbidding people from having any recording items or handheld devices. "If it leaks, then fuck it" was the attitude. When Yeezus finally leaked, it looked like it was done on purpose. However, it was clear from jump that all of these live performances and the anti-stance weren't just conscious decisions for the sake of the art. They were marketing strategies. The album premiered at #1 on the Billboard charts when it was finally made available for purchase.

We can tell ourselves that Jay-Z and other rappers value the art and advancing the art form more than the business, but the industry they're in surely doesn't. The corporations, companies, entities and individuals that they shout out, namedrop, and partner with surely don't. The record labels they record for are most concerned with the bottom line. Rap is nothing more than a product to be marketed and sold to consumers through them. These conglomerates and corporations will employ whatever methods possible to create an event that will ultimately result in the most revenue and the best numbers to report to their shareholders and the business trades. The numbers are all important. The industry was shady. It got taken over. Guess what? It's still shady.

Rappers like Jay-Z hold all the leverage. If they seek to employ you or bring you into the fold, you'd almost be a fool to turn them down. Once you're part of their team, job one is to uphold the brand. Job two is to play your position and contribute/do whatever is asked of you in your particular area of expertise. Job three is simply to wait your turn (if it ever comes, that is). The most valuable piece of currency in business is loyalty. Once your stint is up, you are then free to leave and strike out on your own (I see you Cudi! I see you Hit-Boy!). This is no different from any other business or corporation that acquires startups that may give it competition. For me? Music is as personal as it can possibly get. The thing about business, though, is that it's never personal.

Tags, Throw Ups and Pieces: The Analogy Between Graffiti Writing and Blogging

In the world of graffiti writing, as in the world of blogging, there are different philosophies as how to go from being a "toy" to becoming "All City" or attaining the title of "King". In graffiti, you can bomb relentlessly with tags displaying your unique, opt for "throw ups" to save time and get up quicker and more frequently and when time and space are no issue, or put effort towards banging out a piece or undertaking a fully planned out production.

In the past, in order to truly attain full King status, you had to be able to do all the above. In blogging? Not so much. The ironic part is that when I first started as a writer I specialized in doing tags and throwups, but I simply wasn't gifted enough artistically to pull off full lush production like the ones my favorite writers were capable of. I'm the complete opposite at blogging. I really can't do quick posts. This is as close to a quick post as I get, B….

The tag (or sticker with a tag on it) posted all over the place in graffiti is akin to posting up a pic/pics or an imbedded video on your blog with just a couple of sentences to go along with it. You can do this multiple times a day and draw a gang of eyes to your site, provided you get it up early enough and have people link to it. Difference being that if you're a big enough site, then everyone else will begin posting exactly what you just posted. Not possible in graffiti where you're supposed to have your own individual style and not copy others. Doing that kind of shit will get you fucked up if you ever get caught (and in some cases even bodied).

Next comes the "throw up". It's a mini piece that doesn't take much time or paint to do, and in one night you can do lots of them, whereas you would have to spend all night and use up lots of paint just to do one huge piece or full production. The throw up is analogous to posting up an mp3 or video along with a paragraph to describe or comment on it. This is similar to what I do on Producers I Know when I post a Bandcamp, SoundCloud, Vimeo, or YouTube link with a short explanation of what I posted.

Oftentimes, these throw up kinds of posts on other blogs consist of quick commentary on something that happened recently in pop culture along with a picture on a video link. You give the appearance of putting in serious work without doing the time-consuming research and writing that a full blog/piece would require. Some blogs post between 1-5 times a week and others can post between 25-50. It all depends on what you want to do and what audience you're looking to attract or what style best fits you.

Successfully pulling off the "piece"/"burner" or full production usually requires scouting a time and location to execute, careful planning, a team to finish, a disgusting amount of paint of various colors and a sizable chunk of time, and serious physical exertion and supreme effort. This is why pieces/burners or full productions is are hailed as the gold standard of how to determine who is truly a King or not. If you get busy in EVERY imaginable way I've listed in both disciplines you'll be considered an All Out King.

You can bomb mercilessly with tags, stickers, and throw ups all over the place. But if you can back that up with ill pieces to go along with them? Respect is undeniable. The blog equivalent are these long, well thought-out pieces that people link to all over Twitter and others post a TL: DR on. That's my personal chamber, hence me naming my first blog Poisonous Paragraphs and this the second one Bastard Swordsman. While we all have different approaches to blogging, we must keep in mind that we're all under the same umbrella and to we must remember to keep respect of the culture(s) at the forefront.

Odd Echoes of Bygone Eras: Why The Buzz of Odd Future Was Real

Seemingly from the start, Buzz surrounding the young crew of California rappers and producers collectively known as Odd Future Wolf Gang Kill Them All has spread like wildfire. Not only did Odd Future, as they are more commonly known, amass quite a following among young rap music fans, via free albums released through their own site, OddFuture.com, they also captured the imaginations of hip hop old heads as well. The latter fact is quite intriguing, since we old heads typically hate most new rappers and groups. So why was Odd Future any different?

After Odd Future came out, I'd seen their projects with the weird cover art all over the internet. I'd even heard the names Tyler The Creator, Earl Sweatshirt, Hodgy Beats, Left Brain, and Domo Genesis from time to time form many of my hip hop blogging peers all throughout 2010. However, it wasn't until my boy Has-Lo played a song called "Earl" on the Scrunchface Show and sent me some YouTube and download links to other Odd Future projects and crew members (that I wasn't previously aware of) that I began to really take notice of them.

Once I began listening to various Odd Future offerings at the urging of many of my peers (including Rosalinda), I was instantly engrossed and needed to hear more; but I couldn't exactly pinpoint why at first. After poring through release after release and consistently finding songs that I'd keep on repeat for 15 minutes or more at a time, it finally dawned on me exactly why I (and perhaps a surprising amount of my peers,) was so receptive to Odd Future's music.

It reminded us of the old tried and true Backpack Rap aesthetic all over again. Odd Future was a California based collective of teenagers who not only rhymed and made beats but rode skateboards as well. The best thing about Odd Future is that they developed their own lane and didn't give a fuck. They made their music and released it to the public without worrying if it was going to make a popular blog or if they would get signed by a record label. The industry is was clearly not on their minds when they made music, as 95% of Odd Future's music, when they first came out, wasn't radio friendly.

Oddly enough, the songs that were the least radio friendly were the ones my peers played the most often on their online radio shows. The production perfectly fits the bars of from Odd Future, and the members of the crew could all spit; although there was (is) often dispute as to who in the crew was (is) the nicest and/or the breakout star. This distinction seems to fall on Tyler, the Creator and Earl Sweatshirt. If Odd Future was the Wu Tang Clan when they first hit, then Tyler is RZA and Earl is Method Man.

The two Odd Future projects that my peers seemed to focus on the most are Tyler, the Creator's Bastard and Earl Sweatshirt's Earl. It was surprising and refreshing to see so many older hip hop fans actually embrace some new rappers and producers for once. Especially since Odd Future was not interested in making music that was easily marketable, and they genuinely seemed to hate the media and having us gush over them. Weird, right?

Older heads revealed to me that Odd Future brought them back to when they saw or heard new underground hip hop on Sandbox Automatic, Hip Hop Site, or Underground Hip Hop via RealPlayer clips or on 88HipHop.com. That same feeling of newness, excitement, and discovery they had then, they had again with Odd Future.

That same DIY/independent-as-fuck attitude and aesthetic that made us gravitate to different crews during the Backpack Era

(1997-2002) was fully embodied in the Odd Future's music. The beats didn't sound radio or club ready, and their subject matter and lyrical content is was clearly a byproduct of these teenagers being completely counter to the wave of culture the media had inundated them with their entire conscious lives.

Odd Future's approach to production, recording, and distributing their musical output to the masses might be have been done much the same way that most aspiring artists in 2010 had done, but Odd Future conveyed the same attitude as the crews whose records used to be popular at the iconic hip hop store Fat Beats between 10 to 15 years prior. Ironically, Odd Future was a throwbacks without really trying too hard to be. (Although, in their music they often made references that inferred that they were influenced by this era.)

If you listen to tracks like "Seven," "Assmilk," "Pigions," "Luper," "Sandwitches," "CopKiller," "Super Market," or any other random Odd Future selections, you'll agree that they do did evoke a feeling similar to the indie hip hop songs we copped on vinyl back in the late '90s and early '00s. These tracks could've been recorded on vintage production gear like a Tascam 488 MK II 4-track recorders and produced with EPS 16's or ASR-10's. Back then, Odd Future would have resonated with those fans the same way they do now.

That they had achieved some semblance of success and piqued interest from numerous hip hop blogs, music publications, and record labels, Odd Future still managed to remain skeptical. Some might have wondered how a group of kids spitting misogynistic bars about murder, drugs, violence, and whatever offensive or taboo subject you can think of drew in older hip hop fans. But that's an easy question to answer. We came up listening to Gangsta N.I.P., DMG, Spice-1, Kool G Rap, Nasty Nas, Big L, Akinyele, RA The Rugged Man (Crustified Dibbs), Necro, Cage, Non Phixion, Eminem, and Horrorcore during our formative years. That being the case, we weren't turned off by the subject matter; all it does is remind us of the "good ol' days" of hip hop. In this current era of cats rapping about their material possessions and the nonstop pursuit of fame, money, power, chart position, BDS spins, unit sales, and status it's a breath of fresh air to hear someone say "Fuck you all!" on record. A little nihilism and genuine disgust with the status quo is just what I want to hear right now. We actually need it to be perfectly honest.

Another thing that the rise of Odd Future pointed to, without any intention of doing so, was the complete lack of balance in today's music scene. Whereas back in the days we had a plethora of groups and artists that occupied different lanes and they all could get time on the radio or MTV and BET, those days are now long dead and if we hear anything smacking of originality compared to the dearth of inspiring music that's forced on the masses, there's no question why so many people have responded to Odd Future. That's how and why a gang of foul-mouthed skater kids from California ended up getting embraced by thirty- and forty-something hip hop heads, music bloggers like myself, Khal, Noz, and Combat Jack to Hot 97 radio show hosts like Peter Rosenberg. And to think, they were once pissed off that Nah Right and 2DopeBoyz wouldn't post their material.

With the two main draws being Tyler, the Creator and Earl Sweatshirt, things were made even crazier due to the fact that Tyler became the default group leader because of his age and Earl was sent to boot camp by his mother, which kept from further participating in Odd Future's initial rise. This gives gave MellowHype members Hodgy Beats and Left Brain the opportunity to slide in and occupy the Raekwon and Ghostface Killah role in this ten-men rap ensemble. I'm sure some people felt some trepidation at the Wu Tang Clan comparisons, so I offer you some more that you may be more comfortable with: D.I.T.C, The Great 8 of the Boot Camp Click, Hieroglyphics Crew,

Solesides Crew, Outsidaz, Demigodz, Army Of The Pharaohs, or Weathermen. Any way you word it, Odd Future definitely harkened back to a foregone era and brought with them something that is was sorely lacking in rap music of the early '10s.

17 Days In 1995:
From the Rise of *Only Built 4 Cuban Linx...* to the End of "Yo! MTV Raps"

Nine years ago, I got a call from the homegirl TeLisa D on the first of the month (no Bone Thugz N' Harmony). She told me that she was going to do a special edition of her online radio show ("The B Word") about the 15th anniversary of the release of Raekwon's Only Built 4 Cuban Linx..., and she wondered if I could share some of my memories. Of course, I said yes.

As I called to leave a quick voice message, no more than two minutes, all the memories of that summer day in 1995 that I first heard Only Built 4 Cuban Linx... came rushing back to me. At that time, I'd just graduated high school a few months prior and I was less than three weeks away from my 20th birthday (I'll explain why in the book).

Most of my high school class was getting ready to go to college. I, on the other hand, was working with the Boston Public School and the Office Of The Attorney General doing mediation trainings for $25 an hour. I was saving up to go to college, as I was accepted at Morgan State University in Baltimore, MD. I wouldn't leave Boston until January for the spring semester.

We'd been waiting for Only Built 4 Cuban Linx... to drop for a minute already. Wu-Tang Clan's music was essentially the soundtrack to my time at English High. From the opening bars of "Protect Ya Neck" and the B side "Method Man" to the release of Wu-Tang's debut album, Enter The 36 Chambers, it was as if all of the things that I was immersed in from birth was incorporated in Wu-Tang, both as a group and their music.

The Wu used audio from old Shaw Brothers Ku Fung films, referenced John Woo flicks, namedropped Marvel comic book characters, and even incorporated traditional Chinese legends in their music. These were all things that I was well versed in growing up in South End Boston, right next to Chinatown. Growing up, "Kung Fu Theater" was on television every Saturday afternoon, and comic books were only 25 cents back then.

My senior year of high school was bananas music wise. A number of different big hip hop albums dropped. The Roots's Do You Want More??!", Smif N' Wessun's Dah Shinin, Ol' Dirty Bastard's Return To The 36 Chambers: The Dirty Version, Big L's Lifestyles Ov Da Poor & Dangerous, Masta Ace's Sittin' On Chrome, and Mobb Deep's The Infamous were all the shit up until the end of the school year. Then, Show & AG's Goodfellas dropped right around graduation. We were enjoying a hip hop golden era.

Following the Fresh movie soundtrack, featuring the singles "I Got Cha Back" by GZA and "Heaven & Hell" by Raekwon, anticipation was high for both albums all throughout the year. When the single and videos for "Criminology" and "Glaciers Of Ice" dropped, it was a foregone conclusion that the album Only Built 4 Cuban Linx... was going to be ill. We just had no idea how ill or influential it would become in such a short time.

Only Buit 4 Cuban Linx... dropped back on August 1st, 1995, and I remember being with my boys in a car that one of their girlfriend's owned. We went to the Tower Records down the street from our old apartment on Mass. Ave and we copped the CD, not the cassette tape. Our logic was to go for sound quality and not to take a chance on the cassette tape deck eating it. We stuck that CD in and cruised around Boston and Cambridge all damn day with Only Built 4 Cuban Linx... as our personal theme music.

We copped the album on a Tuesday, yet we rarely (if ever) discussed Soundscan numbers. When we copped the album, none of us ever speculated on how much the jawn would sell or where it would be on the Billboard charts the following week. All we cared about was the overall quality of the album. Keep in mind, we were a bunch of dudes that were aware of the industry, as we were on the radars of many record labels ourselves. It was all about the music and we were fans.

Also keep in mind that "Heaven & Hell," which dropped the previous summer, was still getting radio play, and in June, 1995, both sides of the "Criminology"/"Glaciers Of Ice" single began getting radio play. This meant that three different singles were getting constant burn from an album that had dropped five weeks after the official release of the intended lead single, "Criminology"/"Glaciers Of Ice".

Once the album dropped, I remember heads at radio stations would make their OWN edits of album tracks so they could play them on the air. This was all before the Telecommunications Act Of 1996. Back then, stations still had the freedom and leeway to play what they felt like. They weren't part of a monolithic entity where they were tied to a set playlist yet. I'd hear 'Wu Gambinos" or "Verbal Intercourse" at noon ON THE RADIO less than a week later. It was regular shit then. Completely incomprehensible now.

Here we are, three quarters through one of the greatest years in recent hip hop memory. We're deep in yet another hip hop golden age. We still have a disgusting amount of classic albums yet to drop this same year (GZA's Liquid Swords, AZ's Doe Or Die, and Cypress Hill's Temples Of Boom among them). Son, the world is still 5 five months from even hearing "Fu Gee La" yet! The purple tape (the custom color of the OB4CL... cassette tape) is in decks all over this great nation of ours, but MTV will be airing the final episode of "Yo! MTV Raps" on August 17th, 1995. My 20th birthday. Say word?

It's completely unthinkable that when hip hop was at its zenith, MTV would remove its flagship rap video show from the airwaves. I didn't comprehend it then and I never will. Showbiz &

AG's "Next Level," Junior M.A.F.I.A's "Player's Anthem," Big L's "Street Stuck," Mobb Deep's "Right Back At You," and Ol' Dirty Bastard's "Shimmy Shimmy Ya" were blasting out of everyone's cars. Canceling "Yo! MTV Raps" at that moment was like the Lakers trading away Kobe Bryant, Pau Gasol, Lamar Odom, Andrew Bynum and Ron Artest for cash and draft picks right before the 2010 NBA Playoffs.

This meant that by the time GZA dropped "Cold World," there was no more "Yo! MTV Raps." Fat Joe's "Success" premiered on BET's "Rap City" instead. The videos for Mobb Deep's "Give Up The Goods (Just Step)" and Cypress Hill's "Throw Your Set In The Air," Erick Sermon's "Bomdigi," Jamal's "Fades 'Em All," AZ's "Sugar Hill," and Dogg Pound's "Let's Play House" would never have a chance to air on "Yo! MTV Raps" either. BET's "Rap City" won by default. Problem is, BET wasn't available in every market yet, and the internet was in its infancy.

But here's where the real tragedy lies. Def Jam's 1995 documentary film, The Show, dropped its soundtrack on August 15th, 1995 and the film itself hit theaters on August 20th. Without having MTV in its corner to help promote it to a larger audience the film did dreadfully at the box office. However, the soundtrack to the movie went platinum in two months after release.

The Show soundtrack was powered by the lead single "How High" from Redman & Method Man, which I don't think ever aired on "Yo! MTV Raps" either. How crazy is it to think that MTV removed one of its most influential shows at one of the worst possible times to do so? On the positive side, hip hop videos were stuck added to the regular rotation alongside other genres.

The first time I saw GZA's "Cold World" video on MTV, it was sandwiched between a Veruca Salt, Tricky and a Nine Inch Nails video. I miss those days. Mainstream music didn't suck EITHER. I'll never, for the life of me, forget watching the final episode of "Yo! MTV Raps" and the cipher that occurred. I knew that I was watching history, but I had no grasp of how huge that moment really was at the time. None.

In 17 days, we went from the release of one of the most influential albums of the past 15 years (any genre) to the final episode of one of the most influential shows in the 25+ year history of MTV.

A sort of irony occurred where Raekwon and Ghostface did the knowledge to biters and subliminally dissed Biggie. After Only Built 4 Cuban Linx... dropped, the entire hip hop world bit the Wu. Everyone had aliases. Everyone was a mafioso. Everyone decided to form their own fake Wu Gambino crew.

Eventually, Nas, AZ, Cormega and Foxy Brown would become The Firm (Nature who?). Notorious B.I.G., Jay-Z and Charli Baltimore would become The Commission. Even Common Sense would become Petey Wheatstrow then Willie Stargell. The Wu had already drawn from the film Once Upon A Time In America, so the rest of the rap world would have to seek their own source material.

Credits

All essays in this volume were written by Dart Adams and first published in different versions. Below is a list of the essays along with their previous titles and publication dates.

PART 1

"Hip Hop Has Always Been an Inclusive Art Form and an Exclusive Culture; Mainstream Rap Music Isn't," first published as: Hip-Hop Is Already an Inclusive Artform & an Exclusive Culture. Mainstream Rap Isn't…" at *DJ Booth*, March 5, 2018. Copyright © 2018 S. Adams.

"Hip Hop's Ever Growing Generation Chasm," first published as: "On Rap's Ever Growing Generation Chasm," at *Medium*, June 17, 2014. Copyright © 2014 S. Adams.

1981: The Year Hip-Hop Broke," first published as: "1981: The Year Hip-Hop Broke at *Medium*, June 14, 2016. Copyright © 2016 S. Adams.

1990: Rap's Forgotten Transition Year," first published as: "1990: Rap's Forgotten Transition Year" at *Festivalpeak*, June 15, 2015. Copyright © 2015 S. Adams.

"1991: Rap's Other Forgotten Transition Year," first published as: "1991: Rap's Other Forgotten Transition Year" at *FestivalPeak*, January 9, 2016. Copyright © 2016 S. Adams.

"How The Buzz Around Niki Minaj's Debut Demonstrates the Rap Game Is On Steroids," first published as: "The Rap Game Is On Steroids AKA Dart Adams Is A Fuckin' H8R" at *Bastard Swordsman*, 2011. Copyright © 2011 S. Adams.

"The Quintessential Definition of A Backpacker," first published as: "Mommy, What's A Backpacker? AKA What The Hell Is A Cannibal Ox?" at *Poisonous Paragraphs*, October, 2013. Copyright © 2013 S. Adams.

PART 2

"My J Dilla Journey: A Tale Of Two Jay Dee's; 10 Years Of Fandom vs. 10 Years Of Being A Dilla Scholar (1996–2016)," first published as: "A Tale Of Two Jay Dee's: 10 Years Of Fandom vs. 10 Years Of Being A Dilla Scholar (1996–2016)" at *FestivalPeak*, February 11, 2016. Copyright © 2016 S. Adams.

PART 3

PART 4

Acknowledgments

Dart acknowledges:

I will attempt to name everyone who had a hand in the creation of this book both directly and indirectly over the years. First off, the educator/historian Mel King, Howard Bryant, Bijan C. Bayne, Brian Coleman, Pacey Foster, Adam Mansbach, Chairman Jefferson Mao, FWMJ (stop hane cuh), Megan Ming Francis, Ahmir "Questlove" Thompson, J-Zone, Hex Murda (What up, Hex?), Jean Grae (per usual, you were right), Krishtine de Leon/Rocky Rivera (you were one of my inspirations to pursue journalism in this space), Houseshoes ("Book!"), Davey D (the Raiders are still trash), G. Valentino Ball (thanks for telling me when I was fucking up), Brandon "Bedlam" Matthews (thanks for always telling me the truth), Statik Selektah (since the "spell his name right!" days), Phonte Coleman, Alonzo "Zo!" Ferguson, Rapper Big Pooh, 9th Wonder, Donwill, Von Pea, Pharoahe Monch, DJ Rob Swift, Just Blaze, Double 0, Jose Luis Vilson, Daniel Jose Older, Malka Older, Eve Ewing, Akrobatik ("Remind My Soul" is one of the greatest Rap songs ever made), Edo.G (Thanks for all the gems over the years), DJ 7L & Esoteric/CZARFACE, Bobbito Garcia, Stretch Armstrong, Jonathan Shecter, Peter Nash, Dan Charnas, Shawn Setaro, Amanda Bassa, Kathy Iandoli (Madame Potential with a pencil), Phalary "Pyrex Peas" Long, Skye Brewer, Jazerai Allen-Lord (the realest since '06), Jenee Osterheldt (Black Girl Magic personified), Marlene Boyette (does yoga to GZA's "Liquid Swords), Kianga Lucas, Dutch ReBelle (Kiss Kiss! BANG! BANG!), Marquis Neal, Reggie Charles, DJ Alcide, Big Bear, Yung Paul, DJ Slick Vick, DJ Guru Sanaal, The Architype, Moe Pope, Christopher Talken, Rain, the entire Bridge Sound & Stage staff, CatchWreck, Rob "ProBlak" Gibbs, Ian "LoudMinds" Powell. Simone "Boss Lady" Jordan, Jas Waters, Erika Ramirez, Rae Witte, Sowmya Krishnamurthy, Dana Scott (how much Rap nerdery did we pack into an MIT radio show on a weekly basis?), Alvin "Aqua" Blanco (forever grateful for the opportunity you gave me), Odiesel (thanks for giving me the keys back in the All Hip Hop days), Dallas Penn (Peep the Kirby dots!), Raki Kam (you placing me in T.W.I.B. on Oh Word in back to back weeks meant the world), Eskay (adding me to your blog roll washuge), Khal (since the XXL.com comments section), Talib Kweli (the embodiment of consistency), Donna Disko, Satori Ananda, Meka & Shake (2DBz), Zenobia Simmons, April Walker (your advice was invaluable), DJ Babu, Rhettmatic, J. Rocc, Dam-Funk, Jake One, Mayer Hawthorne, Pete Rock, Grap Luva, 14KT, Elaquent, Dante Ross, Malcolm Gray (the Black Ryan Gosling), Jillian Ducharne, Sofia Snow, Anna Wise, Dane Orr, Danny Brown ("Check!"), Quelle Chris, Black Milk, Rosalinda, Dibia$e, Nassirah Nelson, Denmark Vessey, Havana Joe, Jonathan Kim, Jerry L. Barrow, Karlie Hustle (if you ever need help with your memoir "Thottin' & Boppin'", I'm here), Jay Smooth, John Notarfrancesco, Blame One, Exile, Has-Lo, Michael "ST/MiC" Moxham, Apollo Brown, DJ Soko, Kev Brown, Guy Routte, Jazz Walker (Batman is the greatest superhero ever), Cormega, Large Professor, Kid Cus, Carlito Rodriguez, Cheo Hodari Coker, Sacha Jenkins, Raquel Cepeda, Jeff Chang, Oliver Wang, Hua Hsu, Brian "B+" Cross, Evidence, Rakaa Iriscience, Alchemist, Eric Vanderslice, DJ Disco Wiz, David Dennis Jr., Erin Ashley, Georgette Cline, Tef Poe, Gabriel Teodoros, Tahero Hemphill, Nuri Chandler-Smith, Prince Charles Alexander (your story needs to be told!), Kris Ex, Laurent Fintoni, Dennis de Groot, Henri "My Man Henri" Brisard, Omer Saar, David Dennis Jr,, Martin Douglass, Damien Randle, Chace Infinite, Chris Faraone, Martin Caballero, Brendan McGuirk, Craig Jenkins, Gino Sorcinelli, Yaya Martinez, Meaghan Garvey, Lauren Nostro, Gary Suarez, Yoh Phillips (seeing "The Book Of Yoh" at Harvard's Hip Hop Archive was quite the moment), Dylan "CineMasai" Green, Kno, Dawaun Parker, Phil Beaudreau, Maria "My My" Myraine (7 years of text messages), Naima Cochrane, Toni Morgan, Donna Claire-Chesman, Arielle Gray, Kevin Beacham, Kevin Sekweyama, Geoff "Geespin" Gamere, Frank "The Butcher" Rivera, Christian Ericson, Abigail Bomba (eternal thanks), Ian Steaman, Jasmine Rae Johnson, Sanchay "Dharmic X" Jain, Rachel Klein, Seerat Sohi, Nitz Bluv, Mirin Fader (future legend in the making), Munira Ahmed, Angela Nissel, Ivie Ani, Angelina Navarez, Natalie Crue, Nora Rahimian, Liv Slaughter, Hassan Barclay, Jefe Replay, Rob Kenner, Kevin L. Clark, Dimas Sanfiorenzo, Devin "Dev 1" Horwitz, Bert Haine, Joe Dent, Timmhotep, Eddie "Stats" Houghton, Mike "Big Sto" Stover, Felonious Monk, Vinnie Paz, Jarobi White, Tiffany Probasco, Alexis Claytor, Amar Ediriwira, DJ Spinna, DJ Soul, Kon, DJ Amir, K-Def, Slug of Atmosphere, El-P, Killer Mike & DJ Trackstar (Run The Jewels!), Jake Leidolf, SPNDA, JuneLyfe & the entire SCOPE Apparel gang, the entire Mass Apparel crew,

Joamil Rodriguez and the crew at Laced (what up, Dork!), everyone at Bodega, CNCPTS (salute Deon Point), Sneaker Junkies, AWOL, Alpha & Omega, the staffs at In Your Ear!, Cheapo Records, Vinyl Index, Mark Merren, Devon "Dee Loopz" Guillery and Byran "Art Official Avi" Trench of Stae Tru/Beat Club Podcast, the entire Boston/MA/New England Hip Hop and beat culture scene from The Stew Beat Showcase, Master Of The Machines, The Shift, The Mass Apparel Dojo, The Beat Club Podcast Live & Nightworks alumni and future participants to the crew at Union Sound (I'm looking at you, Loman AKA Juulian Edelman). There's simply too damn many of y'all to list. Salute the entire ST/ShowOff family, Termanology, Easy Money, DJ Deadeye (the glue that keeps it all together), REKS, Supastah Snuk, Chilla Jones, J The S (Idris Clooney forever), Nat Anglin (salute Bos Angeles), Bakari J.B., Jon Tanners, Jay Quarantello, the entire Duck Down massive (what up, James, No Ha & Dru Ha!), Tim Larew (you were right after all), Alexander Richter, Sue Kwon, DJ D-Nice, Peter Caron, Ray Fruschetti, DJ Beanz (BALLET!), Maria Garcia, Simon Rios, Matt Diamond, Christopher Kramer, Cat Morris, Tim Hall, Carl Mello, Clyde Edwards, Miles Marshall Lewis, Neil-Martinez Belkin, Stricklin, Brian "DJ Z" Zisook, Champ Chuck, Magz & the old Overdog Radio crew, Uncle Sam & LFOD Radio staff, Anna Horford, Britni de la Cretaz, Deyscha "Sway" Smith, Morgan Rhodes, D-Stroy, Ales Kot, Russ Bengston, Renee Graham, John Karalis, Jamila Rowser, DJ Benhameen, Tatiana King-Jones, Jamie Righetti, Chico Leo, Lexi Alexander, Lauren Chief Elk, Matthew A. Cherry, Ava DuVernay, The Reel Anderson, Jaislayer, Drewpreme, Premium Pete, Paul Cantor, Bucky Turco, Robert Guinsler, Raydar Ellis, Open Mike Eagle (thanks for mentioning me on "Check To Check"), Mega Ran, Brandon Soderberg (thank you for quoting me in your Spin article), Matt Mason (quoting me in your book changed my life), Eric Coons (forcing me to do radio one night led to my radio career), Gadget (asking me to help A&R a beat tape eventually led to my own label), Sean "Milk" Miliken of IV Boston and Peda Edouard of Mathmatik Athletics (for going in on the Boston Legends brand with me), Amir Ali Said, and last but not least, Said AKA Sa'id (thanks for believing in me back when I didn't see it for myself yet).

This book is dedicated to the memories of Barbara Adams, David Walcott, Alex "Bomba" Rodriguez, Eddie "Smacks" Jackson, Patrice Lassiter, Monique Brown, Richard Jones, J-1 AKA The Deer, Praverb,

Gwarism, Josh The Goon, Voodoo Ray, Reggie "Combat Jack" Osse, Kendric Price, Dave New York, Ras G & Paten Locke.

—Dart

Amir Ali Said acknowledges:

I want to thank my father, Amir Said, for presenting me with this challenge, and for offering his guidance and continued advice. I want to thank Dart for his consistency and for his trust in this collaborative effort. Finally, thank you to Ferguson for his crucial assistance in copyediting and additional support.
—Amir Ali Said

Amir Said acknowledges:

Amir Ali Said, my son, best friend, and Superchamp co-founder, As always, thank you for your friendship, knowledge, courage, and curiosity. Your leadership in this endeavor was impressive and invaluable. Dart, thank you for remaining true and for entrusting me with your work; look forward to our next work together. Géraldine, je te remercie pour tout ! À mercredi ! Christophe, tu es toujours en retard mais tu arrives à l'heure; Valérie, merci beaucoup ! Danny, le 18è hein ? Merci chef.
—Said